The Life and Times of
EDWARD I

OVERLEAF LEFT Edward I with bishops and attendants, from a fourteenth-century manuscript.
RIGHT Bronze ewer in the form of a knight on horseback. *c.* 1300, found in the River Tyne, near Hexham.

BRITISH
MUSEUM

The Life and Times of

EDWARD I

John Chancellor

Introduction by Antonia Fraser

Weidenfeld and Nicolson
London

To my son, Edward

Series designed by Paul Watkins
Filmset by Keyspools Limited, Golborne, Lancashire
Printed in Great Britain by Morrison & Gibb Ltd, Edinburgh and London (A member of the Oxley Printing Group)

Contents

Introduction

'The best lance in all the world' was how the thirteenth-century French troubadours praised Edward I, King of England, making of him their perfect knight, gigantic, strong of soul, never cowed in adversity. Our own picture of Edward I tends to be less romantic: a much bleaker figure is envisaged by that famous epithet painted on his tomb in Westminster Abbey – *Scottorum malleus* – Hammer of the Scots.

Yet it is important to realise the strength of the international prestige enjoyed by Edward I in his own age in order to see his military policies and expenditure in perspective. Nephew by marriage of the French King who has gone down in history as St Louis, Edward was early associated with him in the Eighth (and last) Crusade. After St Louis' death, Edward largely succeeded to his place as European arbiter, this despite the rival claim of the cynical, predatory Philip the Fair. If Edward failed to contain French aggression, at least he aimed at using his prestige to preserve peace in Europe.

At home this unlikely son of the pious and indolent Henry III (and unlikely father of the unfortunate weakling Edward II) was fired by ambition to bring the whole British Isles under one Crown. The result was a country more or less permanently under arms, with grave financial problems. One should, however, judge his actions against the Welsh and Scots – and the Jews, whom he finally expelled from the country – in their context: this was the age of the Crusades, and to Edward these were so many crusades, by which he fulfilled his coronation oath.

More sympathetic to us today is his great work as a lawgiver. The King who was termed the 'English Justinian' may have intended merely to establish the rights of the Crown over those of the barons; but the result was the great years of the statutes from 1274 to 1290, when the English legal system, as it had grown up, was deliberately grouped together and codified. As for Parliament, Edward I, for all that Simon de Montfort fell at his hands at Evesham in 1265, has been aptly described as Montfort's true heir in trusting the judgment of the people at large.

It is significant that this warrior King enjoyed an exceptionally happy marriage, although admittedly his much-loved consort Eleanor of Castile was obliged to become a more or less permanent camp follower; the births of several of his large family of children, including that of the future Edward II, being 'campaign deliveries'. The love which Edward bore for Eleanor was poignantly commemorated after her untimely death by the twelve Eleanor Crosses which marked the places where her bier rested on its progress to her royal funeral.

John Chancellor gives us a balanced and compelling portrait of a man whose achievements dazzled his contemporaries, many of which still have the power to win our interest and admiration.

Antonia Fraser

Acknowledgments

Photographs and illustrations were supplied or are reproduced by kind permission of the following. The picture on page *147* is reproduced by gracious permission of Her Majesty The Queen. The picture on page 191 is reproduced by permission of His Grace the Archbishop of Canterbury and the Trustees of Lambeth Palace Library; Aerofilms Limited: 187; J. Allan Cash: 61, 90–1, 99, 114, 117, 119, 189, 192, 207, 210; Archivo Municipal, Burgos (photo MAS): 31; Archives Nationales, Paris: 166; Batsford: 108; Biblioteca Apostolica, Vaticana: 39, 159; Biblioteca Estense, Modena: 87; Bibliothèque Nationale, Paris: 24 (photo Bisonte/Sara Ellis), 58–9, 153 (photo Bisonte/Sara Ellis); Bodleian Library, Oxford: 34–5 (MS Douce 180 f31), 72–3 (MS Tanner 190 f204v, 205r), 79 (MS Tanner 190 f22r),88 (MS Tanner 190 f189v), 133 *above*, 134 (MS Hatton 10 f50r), 141 *above* (MS Douce 48 f18v), 141 *below*, 208–9 (MS Auct. D.3.2.f238r), 216 (MS Rawl. C292 f9r); British Library: *2*, 17, 18, 25, 26, 36, 50 *below*, 51, 53, 57, 62, 70, 77 (photo Courtauld Institute of Art), *89*, 94–5 (photo Courtauld Institute of Art), 102 (photo Courtauld Institute of Art), 111, 132 *above*, 136, *150–1*, *154–5*, 188, *193*; British Museum: *3*, 55, 133 *below*; The Master and Fellows of Christ Church, Oxford: 212; The Master and Fellows of Corpus Christi College, Cambridge (photo Courtauld Institute of Art): 103; Department of the Environment: 127; Stanley Eost and P. Macdonald: 22; Fitzwilliam Museum, Cambridge: 40–1 (photo Hamlyn Picture Library), 64–5, 67, *85*, 105, 139, 179; Werner Forman: 12–13, *15*, *196*; Giraudon: 58–9, 82, 83, 156–7, 160, 166; Glasgow University Library: 175; Angelo Hornak: *14*; © Masters of the Bench of the Inner Temple (photo e t archives): *146*; A.F. Kersting: *96*, 97 *above*, 120–1; Mansell: 84, 144, 177; Monasterio del Escorial, Madrid (photo MAS): 28, 29;

National Galleries of Scotland: 194; National Library of Scotland: 198; National Monuments Record: 130, 203; Picturepoint: *93, 205*; Public Record Office: 137, 168; Sir David Ogilvy, Bart. (photo National Library of Scotland): 184, 185; Radio Times Hulton Picture Library: 122, 140; Scala: 87; Walter Scott: 217; Scottish Record Office: 172–3; Edwin Smith: 97 *below*; Snark International: 69, *81*; Trinity College, Cambridge: 132 *below*; A. Vaughan Kimber: 148, 200, 201; Roget Viollet: 170; Victoria and Albert Museum, London: 45; Warburg Institute (photo National Monuments Record): 46; Weidenfeld and Nicolson Archives: 50 *above*, 158; Dean and Chapter of Westminster: 21.

Numbers in italics indicate colour illustrations

Picture research by Caroline Lucas
Maps drawn by Patrick Leeson

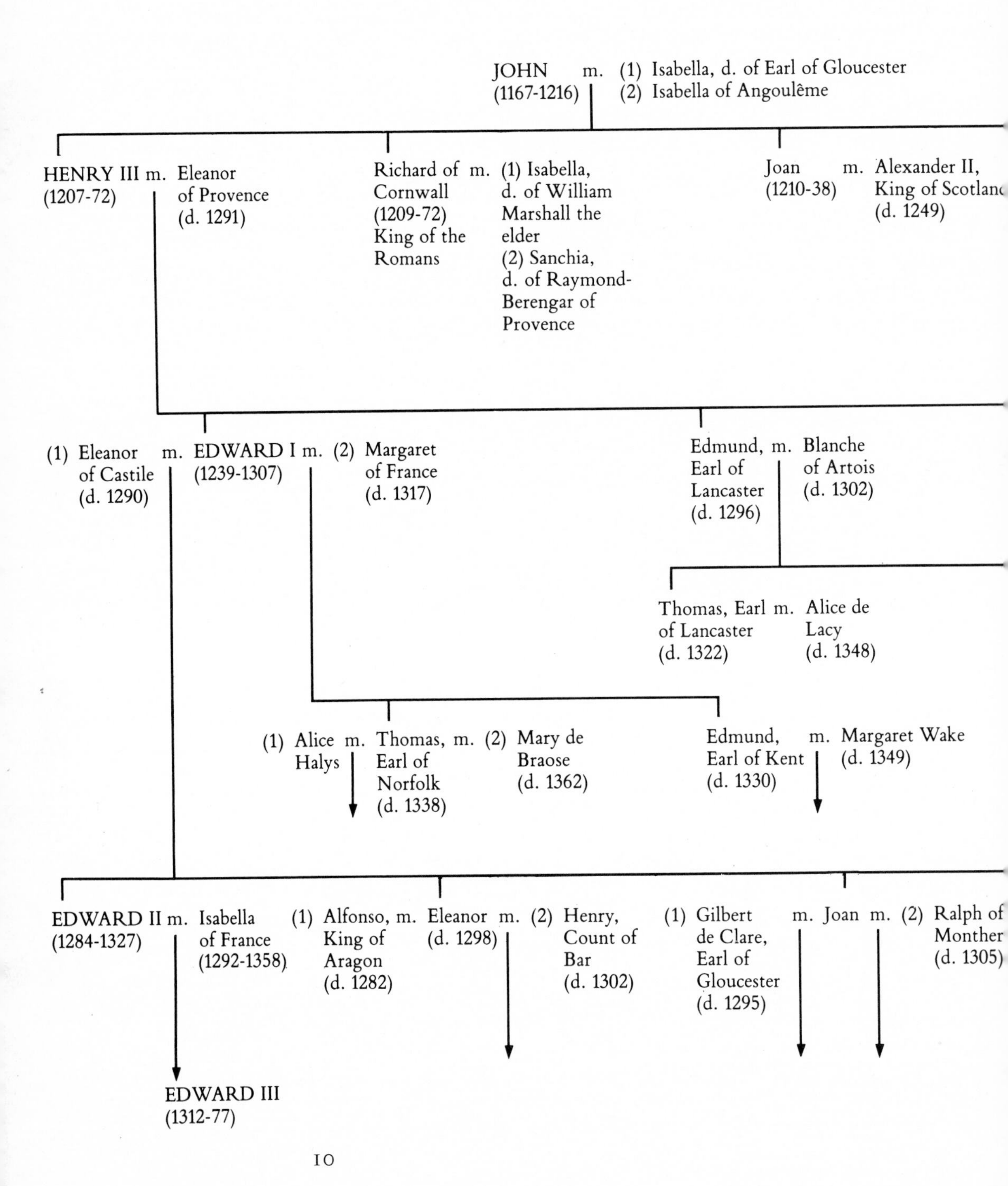
JOHN (1167-1216) m. (1) Isabella, d. of Earl of Gloucester (2) Isabella of Angoulême
HENRY III (1207-72) m. Eleanor of Provence (d. 1291)
Richard of Cornwall (1209-72) King of the Romans m. (1) Isabella, d. of William Marshall the elder (2) Sanchia, d. of Raymond-Berengar of Provence
Joan (1210-38) m. Alexander II, King of Scotlan (d. 1249)
(1) Eleanor of Castile (d. 1290) m. EDWARD I (1239-1307) m. (2) Margaret of France (d. 1317)
Edmund, Earl of Lancaster (d. 1296) m. Blanche of Artois (d. 1302)
Thomas, Earl of Lancaster (d. 1322) m. Alice de Lacy (d. 1348)
(1) Alice Halys m. Thomas, Earl of Norfolk (d. 1338) m. (2) Mary de Braose (d. 1362)
Edmund, Earl of Kent (d. 1330) m. Margaret Wake (d. 1349)
EDWARD II (1284-1327) m. Isabella of France (1292-1358)
(1) Alfonso, King of Aragon (d. 1282) m. Eleanor (d. 1298) m. (2) Henry, Count of Bar (d. 1302)
(1) Gilbert de Clare, Earl of Gloucester (d. 1295) m. Joan m. (2) Ralph of Monther (d. 1305)
EDWARD III (1312-77)

House of Plantagenet

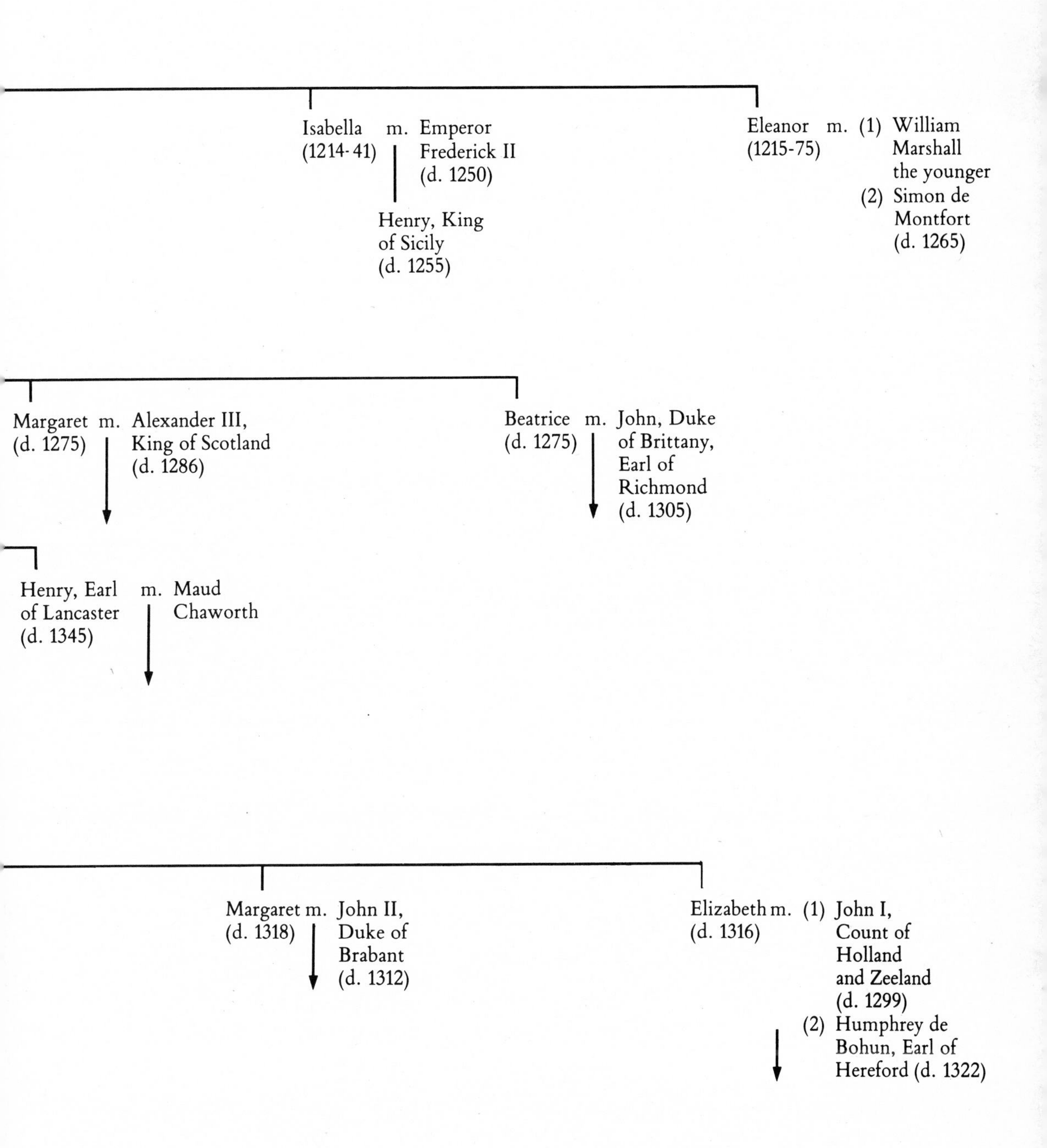

Isabella (1214-41) m. Emperor Frederick II (d. 1250)
Henry, King of Sicily (d. 1255)
Eleanor (1215-75) m. (1) William Marshall the younger (2) Simon de Montfort (d. 1265)
Margaret (d. 1275) m. Alexander III, King of Scotland (d. 1286)
Beatrice (d. 1275) m. John, Duke of Brittany, Earl of Richmond (d. 1305)
Henry, Earl of Lancaster (d. 1345) m. Maud Chaworth
Margaret (d. 1318) m. John II, Duke of Brabant (d. 1312)
Elizabeth (d. 1316) m. (1) John I, Count of Holland and Zeeland (d. 1299) (2) Humphrey de Bohun, Earl of Hereford (d. 1322)

1 Father and Son 1239-54

PREVIOUS PAGES The head of Henry III from the gilt-bronze effigy by William Torel in Westminster Abbey.

ABOVE Detail of the gilt-bronze canopy and head of Eleanor of Castile, made by William Torel for Eleanor's tomb in Westminster Abbey.

OPPOSITE Part of the painted sedilia to the right of the high altar in Westminster Abbey erected during the reign of Edward I. This detail shows a king, possibly Henry III or Edward I.

HENRY III chose the name of Edward for his eldest son in honour of his favourite saint, Edward the Confessor (1042–66), the last Anglo-Saxon king and son of Ethelred the Unready. Henry had since boyhood venerated the Confessor, to whom he bore a certain resemblance. Both were pious and indolent, with a taste for building; both had cosmopolitan Courts and lavished favours on foreigners whom they preferred to their own countrymen; both were devious, weak, irresponsible and spiteful; and yet both at the end of their long reigns (although Henry's was more than twice as long as that of Edward) left their country richer and more stable than when they had inherited it. Henry may have felt united to the Confessor by these common personal traits. His domestic life was at least more wholesome. The Confessor was harsh to his wife and mother and is said never to have consummated his marriage. A later chronicler said of him, 'His virtues would

have adorned a cloister; his failings ill became a throne.' Pope Alexander III was persuaded to canonise him in 1161, an event which lent encouragement to the cult of the royal saint.

Both the Confessor and Henry III pulled down and rebuilt Westminster Abbey, leaving buildings of unexampled splendour by English standards. The Confessor's new Norman church was copied from the Abbey of Jumièges near Rouen, and Henry III's Gothic church was very like some of the great cathedrals which had been rising in the Ile de France during the thirteenth century – 'a French thought expressed in English idiom', as Gilbert Scott put it. The Confessor had rebuilt the Abbey on a grand scale; he intended it, so it is thought, to be the place of burial for himself and his heirs and to be the scene for future coronations. William the Conqueror and his heirs were anxious to appear as the natural and legitimate successors of the Saxon royal line and, on the pretext of reigning according to the Confessor's will, they encouraged the claims of Westminster to be at once the royal crowning place and burial ground. The canonisation of the dead Edward gave great impetus to these claims and it was not long before the monks in the Abbey had made a collection of vestments, sceptres, a crown and other finery which were immediately accepted as the regalia of the sainted King and became the regalia of the English kings at their coronations.

In 1245 Henry III embarked on the greatest architectural enterprise of his reign – the rebuilding of Westminster Abbey. His twin motives were personal piety and aesthetic ambition. Whatever the many failures, miseries and follies of his long reign (1216–72), this great achievement testifies to certain qualities in a King whom Bishop Stubbs describes as being, unlike his son, 'utterly devoid of all the elements of greatness'. His qualities were not dissimilar to those possessed by Charles I: liberality, magnificence, a refined mind and cultivated tastes. One could say that the liberties enjoyed by the English are to some extent due to the political foolishness of their art-loving kings. On the Continent, architecture and the decorative arts were used by kings, for example Louis XIV, as expressions and

OPPOSITE Henry III enthroned, from Matthew Paris' *Historia Anglorum*. In one hand the King holds a sceptre, in the other a model of his new Abbey Church at Westminster.

Medieval building techniques as depicted in a thirteenth-century manuscript.

instruments of political power. With Henry III, patronage of the arts was a substitute for political incapacity. He took refuge in building and in schemes of decoration which made his reign as famous in the history of art as it is inglorious in that of the monarchy. 'Westminster Abbey is the truest memorial to a King who was a better judge of sculpture and painting than he was of politics and men.'

What distinguishes Henry from all other English kings is the personal interest which he took not only in the building and maintenance of his houses, castles and those churches and abbeys which he endowed or founded, but also in the outward tokens of kingship such as thrones, crowns, seals and banners. However irresolute politically, he was always determined to gratify his highly developed aesthetic sense. He would let nothing stand in the way of the execution of a building project or scheme of decoration. At one period eight hundred men were working on the construction of Westminster Abbey. Henry's impecuniosity and the terrible years of civil war (1264–7) did not deflect him from the project. He undertook to finance personally the building of the new Abbey Church. In a papal bull in 1245 Innocent IV had called on the faithful to help with their contributions to rebuild a church which was 'very old and decayed'. Private benefactions did not, however, come to much and at one stage Henry was driven to the terrible extremity of having to pawn the jewelled treasures on the unfinished shrine of the Confessor.

This golden shrine was Henry's pride and joy. Ever since he had been crowned in 1220, at the age of thirteen, in the Confessor's church, he had wanted to raise a monument to his patron saint. Henry concentrated his profoundest feelings on the construction of the shrine: his veneration for the Confessor, his fondness for ceremonial and his love of art as exemplified in his passion for gold and silver, for jewels and enamels, for curiously wrought sacred vessels, for marbles and cameos and embroidered vestments. Had he concentrated his mind upon affairs of state as successfully as he did upon works of art, remarked one biographer, he might have been the greatest of our kings.

The Confessor's Day, 13 October, was for Henry III the great day of the year and he used the occasion to satisfy his artistic interests and his love of ceremonial. On 13 October 1269 there took place the solemn translation of the Confessor's remains from his tomb behind the high altar to their newly completed shrine. They were carried on the shoulders of the King, his

OPPOSITE Rudolf Ackermann's engraving of the shrine of Edward the Confessor in Westminster Abbey, 1812, The shrine survives today in a much mutilated form, having been stripped of its gold casing and mosaic decorations during the dissolution of the monasteries in the sixteenth century.

brother Richard of Cornwall, King of the Romans, and his sons, Edward and Edmund. (Despite Henry's predilection for everything French, this did not stop him choosing Anglo-Saxon names for both his sons.) This was for Henry the greatest moment of his reign; for over twenty years he had been absorbed in the smallest details of the new work at Westminster.

Little now remains of the golden shrine. On that famous day when the sacred remains were placed in it, mass was said for the first time in the new church and afterwards a great feast was held in the adjoining palace to celebrate the occasion. A few months later, in August 1270, Edward left to join Louis IX (St Louis), King of France, on Crusade. Father and son were never to see each other again. Henry died at Westminster on St Edmund's Day, 16 November 1272, when Edward was on his way home from the Holy Land. Four days later, on 20 November, Henry's body was placed in the tomb behind the high altar from which the Confessor's bones had been removed. Henry's veneration of the Confessor was far from being a whimsical private cult: all later Plantagenets were anxious to be positioned as near as possible to the shrine of St Edward, and Henry certainly deserved to lie near his favourite saint. In 1290 his coffin was moved to a new tomb on the north side of the shrine. The other tombs to the north of the Confessor's chapel are those of Edward I and of his wife, Queen Eleanor.

The tombs of father and son are not at all alike and may be taken as illustrative of two quite different temperaments and personalities. Edward's tomb is a great plain chest of black Purbeck marble without any kind of adornment whatsoever; it had neither an effigy nor an engraved inscription. Many years later an inscription was painted on his tomb containing the epithet *Scottorum malleus* (Hammer of the Scots) and the motto *Pactum serva* (Keep troth). Did Edward, who adorned the tombs of his father and his wife so magnificently, wish himself to be remembered by this simple and unprepossessing monument? It has certainly encouraged later generations' one-sided picture of him as a stern, laconic warrior and lawgiver. What is more probable is that his son, undutiful in his father's lifetime and

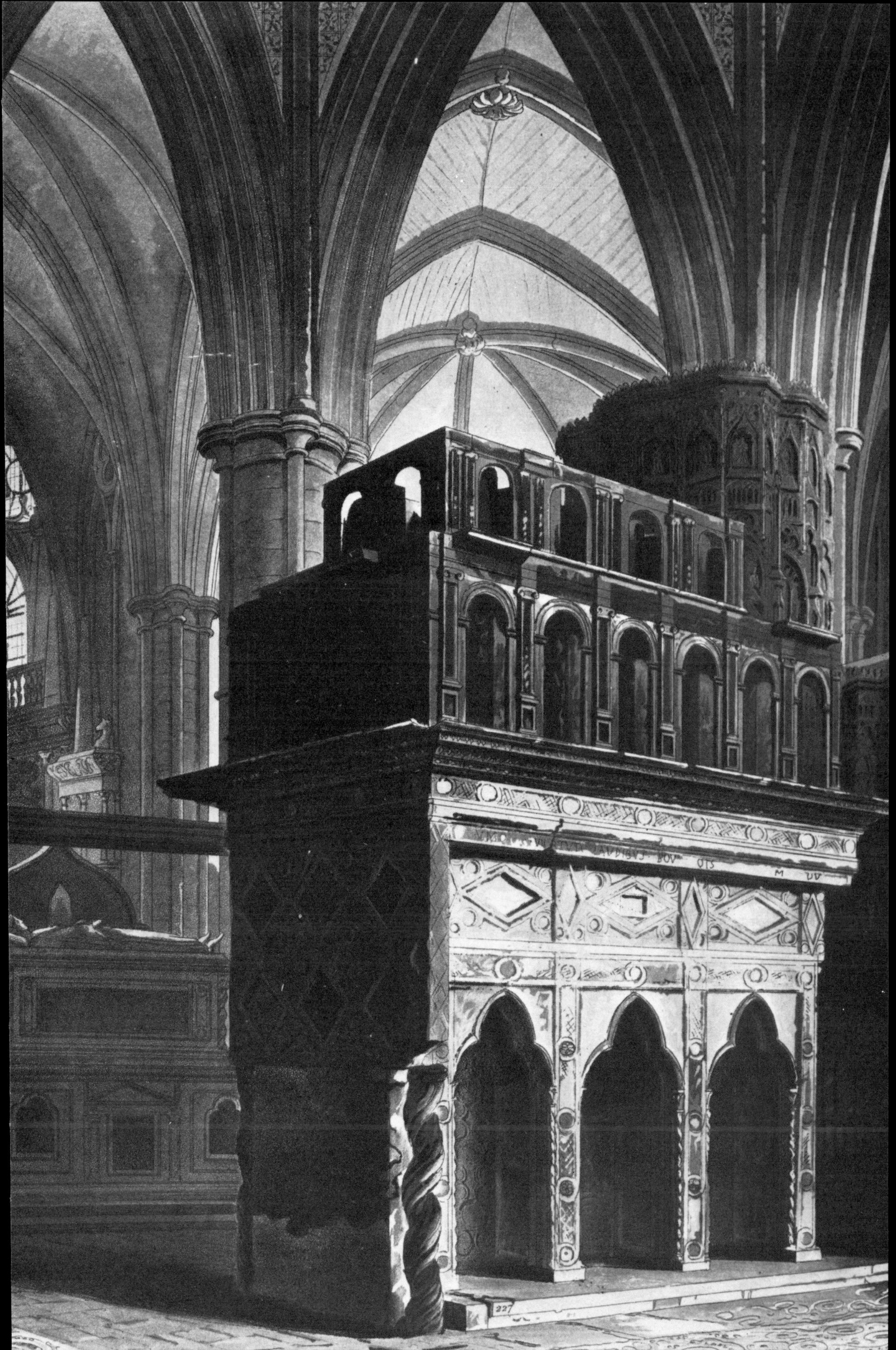

neglectful after his death, chose to do no more than convention demanded. Although no contemporary documents about the tomb have been preserved, we do know that year after year, throughout the fourteenth and fifteenth centuries, the Exchequer paid the sacrist of Westminster to keep wax candles burning 'round the body of the Lord Edward, formerly King of England, of famous memory'.

Henry's tomb, on the other hand, which he may well have commissioned himself, is an expression of his lavish, artistic tastes. Made by Peter the Roman, one of the Italian *marmorani* that Henry delighted to employ, it is of Purbeck marble with Italian marble inlay and marble and glass mosaics. Edward later had precious stones brought over from France to beautify his father's tomb. Later still, in 1291, the tomb was completed by William Torel's gilt-bronze effigy. It was Torel, a London goldsmith, who also made the exquisite effigy of Edward's beloved wife Eleanor – one of the most perfect of all monuments to medieval royalty.

Edward was born at Westminster in June 1239. He was baptised a few days later and Simon de Montfort, who was married to the King's sister Eleanor, was one of his godfathers. Henry made it clear that this joyous occasion should be celebrated by many handsome gifts to himself. If they did not come up to expectations, he returned them and asked for something better. 'God gave us this infant, but our Lord the King sells him to us,' said the cynical Londoners.

All biographers of Henry III are in agreement that, whatever his other personality weaknesses, he was himself a model of domestic virtue. His children were brought up in an atmosphere of purity and piety. Henry attended three masses a day, which even his brother-in-law, St Louis, thought excessive. Dante called him *'il Re della simplice vita'*, and placed him in a valley where those sat who had not been evil but who had been careless of the great reward. As we have seen, the virtuous moral life of the royal family did not go hand in hand with a Quaker simplicity of living. Henry liked to live

OPPOSITE The tomb of Henry III in Westminster Abbey. William Torel's gilt-bronze effigy of the King is set upon a high plinth made by Peter the Roman, decorated with mosaic and set with slabs of porphyry.

A king and queen feasting with their court, from a late thirteenth-century French manuscript.

splendidly and to entertain lavishly; he spent enormous sums on decorating his many manors, castles and palaces, particularly Westminster, Winchester, Windsor and Woodstock. He liked big house-parties and ceremonial feasts, especially when they were attended by his foreign kinsmen and their hangers-on. He was disastrously attached to the family of his wife, Eleanor of Provence, who encouraged the rapacity of her relatives.

Henry's patronage of foreign adventurers who were totally unfitted for spiritual or administrative offices in England earned him the severe disapproval of Matthew Paris, the St Albans monk and historian whose chronicle of the times of Henry III ends abruptly in 1259, when Edward was twenty years old. His writings give us an admirable background to the world in which Edward grew up. He describes the struggle between the Empire and the papacy, the Crusades and other movements in the eastern Empire, as well as events in England. Although he liked Henry, he was deeply angered by his propensity for appointing foreigners to high places in Church and State.

Thoroughly patriotic and a believer in freedom, he spared neither king nor pope whenever he saw an instance of foreign abuse of national interests. The writings of this educated and honest chronicler shed a vibrant light on Henry's confused and mediocre reign; he emerges from them a bad king with many reprehensible weaknesses of character, but also with many endearing human traits. Edward's reign and character are that much more obscure for lacking a chronicler to record them with humour and objectivity.

A self-portrait of Matthew Paris from his *Chronica Majora*. The chronicles of this St Albans monk bring to life many of the great events and characters of the first half of the thirteenth century.

Eleanor of Provence, surnamed 'La Belle', the mother of Edward I, Edmund, Earl of Lancaster, Margaret, wife of King Alexander III of Scotland, and Beatrice, wife of John, Duke of Brittany and Earl of Richmond, was one of several beautiful daughters of Raymond-Berengar IV, Count of Provence. Her sister, Margaret, was married to St Louis of France. Eleanor brought with her to England a whiff of the culture of that land of song and poetry. Both her parents figured amongst the Provençal poets and Eleanor herself composed an heroic poem

Henricus Rex anglie genuit
Edwardum Regem Anglie
Edmundum Comitem Leicestrie
Margaretam Reginam Scotie
Beatricem Comitissam Britannie
Alexandri qui obiit
Petrus et Iohannes

in her native language when still a child. Henry loved her uxoriously and feebly bestowed titles, estates and bishoprics upon her relations. This made her, so Agnes Strickland in *The Lives of the Queens of England* tells us, 'the most unpopular queen that ever presided over the court of England'. She encouraged Henry in his extravagant spending on interior decoration, fine clothes and jewels; and she had a taste for political power which Henry unwisely allowed her to gratify. Yet she was a good and affectionate mother, however imperious outside the family circle. Edward remained attached to her throughout her life and when, as a widow, she retired to Amesbury and took the veil, he continued to visit her.

Little is known of the upbringing of Edward and his brother and sisters. More manly and sporting in his tastes than his father, he assimilated some of the culture and piety of his civilised parents and of their artistic and cosmopolitan court. He received the disciplined education of a thirteenth-century prince: he could read and write Latin and French, he was trained in the arts and sciences, in music and versification. He learned about the world in general while listening to discussions in Council and at Court, while hunting and travelling. He discovered early in life the duties of a prince and the nature and functions of political power. He was to become for his countrymen and contemporaries, at home and abroad, a real knight, a gigantic, fine, fierce creature, strong of soul and never cowed in adversity.

Despite their very different characters and the Plantagenet tradition of family feuds, there existed a strong affection between Edward and his father. There is a story of the fourteen-year-old Edward unable to control his sobs as he watched Henry set sail for Gascony with three hundred ships in the hope of succeeding, where his viceroy and brother-in-law, Simon de Montfort, had failed, in restoring that rebellious dukedom to obedience. There is another story of how Henry in 1260, convinced that Edward was plotting with Simon to overthrow him during his absence in France, returned in a fury to England and summoned his son to his presence. 'The moment I see him', he said, 'I shall embrace and forgive him' – which he did.

OPPOSITE Henry III portrayed with one of the churches which he built, from the *Chronicle of England* by Peter Langtoff.

King Alfonso x, the Wise, half-brother of Eleanor of Castile. His renunciation of all claims to Gascony was the chief reason for the arranged marriage between the nine-year-old Eleanor and fifteen-year-old Edward.

Edward's education has been described as a long struggle, on the one hand, to remedy his father's errors and, on the other, to humble his father's enemies. He would probably have agreed with those historians who have heaped Henry's memory with opprobrious epithets – a moral coward, false, shifty, unreliable, infirm of purpose, un-English in feeling, letting his Provençal and Poitevin relations swarm the Court and live off the country; a man without the slightest talent for administration and completely lacking in political commonsense. It was probably Edward's knowledge of his father's weaknesses that determined him to be a strong prince, to 'keep troth', honour agreements and be loyal to his friends. A less desirable result of the reaction against his father's opportunism and untruthfulness was his recourse in awkward situations to a narrow and disingenuous legal pedantry. It must have been agonising for the manly, realistic Edward to sit back and witness the hideous result of his father's countless acts of folly – nine years of civil turmoil – without reproaches, knowing that it probably spelt the end of his own inheritance. His exemplary loyalty, coupled

Musical entertainment at the Court of Alfonso x.

with his decisive behaviour, was to be rewarded when he inherited in 1272 a loyal, prosperous and united country.

Edward's first introduction to public life came in 1254 when he sailed from Portsmouth with his mother and her uncle Boniface of Savoy, Archbishop of Canterbury, to Bordeaux. He was just fifteen and on his way to meet and to marry Eleanor of Castile, the half-sister of the philosopher King Alfonso x (the

Wise) of Castile. They crossed the Pyrenees and travelled to Burgos, the capital of Castile: Edward and Eleanor married at the Monastery of Las Huelgas, on the edge of Burgos, at the end of October. Alfonso knighted him and solemnly renounced all claims to Gascony, which had been the dowry of his great-grandmother. This renunciation was the main reason for this arranged marriage, which turned out to be one of history's love-matches, commemorated by the Eleanor Crosses, those touching monuments erected to a wife by her bereaved husband.

Shortly before Edward's marriage his father had given him Gascony, the whole of Ireland (except Dublin and Limerick), Wales, Chester, Bristol, Stamford, Grantham and the Channel Islands. He guaranteed Edward a minimum income of 15,000 marks a year. Edward was indeed an eligible match. He had, at the age of fifteen, his own household, a huge income, and properties as large if not larger than those of his father. He was almost king already; in Gascony, however, his powers were limited by his father's supervision. Having divested himself of all these possessions, Henry went to Paris to be royally entertained by his brother-in-law, St Louis, and to study the model of the Sainte-Chapelle. He was so delighted by the church and it gave him so many ideas for Westminster Abbey that he wanted, we are told, to put it in a cart and bring it back to England.

For Henry III, whose tastes were more French than English, who was himself almost entirely French, whose wife and closest friends were French, the lost Angevin Empire of the English kings was a heartbreaking matter. For once, he himself was not to blame. By the time he came to the throne, France was no longer a geographical expression but the most powerful state in Europe. This was the achievement of Philip Augustus (1180–1223), who successfully exploited the political folly of Richard I and his brother, John. During Philip Augustus's reign the monarchy in France was transmuted from theory into fact. He annexed Normandy, Artois, Maine, Anjou and Touraine, and his son, Louis VIII, in his turn conquered Poitou. The duchy

Two Castilian knights from a fourteenth-century Spanish manuscript. Their shields bear the arms of Laon and Castile.

of Gascony was all that remained of the once-vast French possessions of the English king. The name Gascony came from the Gascones who plundered and then settled the area between the Pyrenees and the Garonne. After the break-up of the Carolingian Empire, it was ruled by an independent line of dukes who annexed various counties such as Bordeaux, Agen and Bazas. In the eleventh century Gascony became united with the duchy of Aquitaine which was centered on Poitou. These two duchies were inherited by Eleanor of Aquitaine, wife of Henry II, who ruled the whole area as Duke of Aquitaine. After the English lost Poitou, Henry III continued to rule as Duke of

Aquitaine and his son Edward inherited the title. Gascony came to have the same symbolic importance for Henry that Calais had for Mary Tudor; he clung to the beautiful, ungovernable duchy with a furious tenacity. The retention of this remnant of his father's Continental lordships concentrated his mind as did the rebuilding of Westminster Abbey. At least Henry did not lose the duchy: it remained in English hands until 1451.

The history of Gascony under English rule is a welter of feudal complexities, of conflicting rights and claims to vassalage and inheritance. The duchy was in permanent jeopardy from forces within and without. Within were the great vassals, and without were the kings of France, still bent on the abasement of the House of Anjou and the assertion of their rights over vassals, and the kings of Castile. Henry had sent his formidable brother-in-law, Simon de Montfort, in 1248 to restore order in the turbulent duchy; in 1252 Henry, lending a willing ear to Simon's enemies, had him tried at Westminster for corruption and mismanagement. The Earl was exonerated but dismissed, and Henry sailed with three hundred ships to try to create order in the duchy. This was the occasion when Edward sobbed as he watched the sails of his father's ships disappear over the horizon. By means of the marriage of Edward to Eleanor and his friendship with St Louis, Henry hoped to secure Gascony against its most dangerous neighbours and, by a policy of conciliation, to curb the restlessness of the Gascon barons. Then, having settled Gascony and handed over to Edward his new lordship, he intended to go on Crusade. With this scheme in mind, he had taken the cross in 1250.

Edward stayed in Gascony for a year after his marriage, studying the administration of the duchy which was in the hands of his seneschal and the Constable of Bordeaux. Later, as King, he took Gascon affairs very seriously, making two long stays there – from 1273 to 1274 and from 1286 to 1289 – building castles, as he had done in Wales and southern Scotland, and improving the administration. Meanwhile, Henry had characteristically let his crusading ardour be diverted by the fatal lure of the Sicilian Crown. The 'Sicilian Business', as the adventure came to be called, was to lead to the Treaty of Paris (1259) with St Louis, which brought to a formal end the Angevin Empire. It precipitated the King's surrender to a committee of barons in 1258, which was followed by nine years of civil turmoil and the confrontation between Henry and Edward on the one hand, and their great adversary, Simon de Montfort, on the other. The impending crisis was to teach Edward some lessons which he would remember for the rest of his life.

2 The Lord Edward 1254-65

THE DAY OF RECKONING was approaching for Henry III. Until the year 1258 he was in undisputed charge of the country and during much of that period he had tasted the sweet fruits of absolute power. Thanks not to him, but to his many able officials and to the steady development of legal and administrative changes initiated by his grandfather Henry II, the authority and efficiency of the central, or royal, government had been established in every part of the country by the middle of the thirteenth century.

Henry showed himself to be totally unfit for the enormous power and responsibility which the increased centralisation of government had placed in his hands. The reasons for the Barons' Revolt and the subsequent drastic and revolutionary curbing of royal power are not to be found, as is sometimes said,

PREVIOUS PAGES A scene from the pro-royalist, thirteenth-century *Douce Apocalypse*. The banner of the attacking knights bears a lion rampart, the arms of Simon de Montfort. On the death of Edward I his knights lamented one under whose leadership 'we plucked the Kingdom of England from the mouth of the lion, when we freed Daniel, King Henry III, from the hand of the beast in the war of Evesham'.

RIGHT Henry III from a History of England by the monks of St Albans, *c.* 1403.

in defects of government and administration, but in the character and policies of Henry himself.

Henry's culminating act of folly, which ushered in the Barons' War and the constitutional quarrels and developments of the next ten years, was the Sicilian Business. In 1254 Pope Innocent IV offered Henry the throne of Sicily which he accepted on behalf of his nine-year-old son, Edmund. Henry, as we have seen, was not a strong king: he was romantic, unrealistic, easily distracted and took things at their face value. What could be more delightfully irrelevant to the needs of his country than to place his small son on an Italian throne?

The offer of the Sicilian Crown arose out of the continuous and bitter disputes between the papacy and the German emperors throughout the twelfth and thirteenth centuries for the domination of the Italian states. The gradual erosion of that great ideal of a united Christendom under the joint guidance of the spiritual and temporal powers was a tragic feature of the history of the later Middle Ages. The grotesque disparity between the pretensions of the great offices of pope and emperor and the human failings of their holders explains only too well the narrow, selfish and cynical attitudes of the rulers of the European nation states.

In the twelfth century, the dramatic confrontation between pope and emperor found its expression in the so-called 'Investiture Contest', which culminated in the humiliation of the Emperor at Canossa, when Henry IV waited three days barefoot outside the castle walls before Gregory VII (Hildebrand) consented to receive him and give him absolution. The popes, in claiming that they had received from Christ the authority to depose any earthly ruler, and in exercising that right in the case of the German emperor, dealt a shattering blow to the unity of Germany and to the mystical alliance of Empire and papacy. Once the emperor had lost the moral and legal right to designate his successor, then the German Crown became an object of intrigue and barter. As France and England developed their centralised monarchies, Germany tore itself to pieces in dynastic feuds and wars.

Thanks to their strong territorial base in south-western Germany and to their great abilities, the Dukes of Swabia of the family of Hohenstaufen managed to secure the German Crown in the twelfth century. Frederick Barbarossa was the first Hohenstaufen emperor, whose son Henry (later the Emperor Henry VI and father of Frederick II) made that ominous marriage with Constance, heiress of the kingdom of Sicily which included southern Italy. Three generations of Hohenstaufen pursued with single-minded fervour the imperial ideal, which meant in practical terms the unification of all Germany and Italy under the imperial Crown.

The Emperor Frederick II, like his father the Emperor Henry VI before him, wished to transmute the ideal of the Holy Roman Empire into a reality. Although this extraordinary man gave the impression that he was succeeding in his aim, the odds were against him and, when he died, the imperial policy was in ruins. He had lacked what he most needed to impose his authority in the west – the support of a loyal and united Germany. Disputed elections and the resulting civil wars in the twelfth and thirteenth centuries had discredited the imperial ambition, just as the readiness of the popes to step down from the throne of St Peter and embroil themselves in territorial disputes had tarnished the spirituality of the papacy. The dukes and princes of Germany were bent on enlarging their own domains and the last thing they wanted was a strong king who would have the power to call them to order. They found in the pope an unexpected ally, for both wished, for their own reasons, to have a weak king-emperor.

According to papal theory, the king of Sicily was the pope's vassal and the pope could dethrone him, if he so wished. Innocent IV had, in 1245, deposed and banned for sacrilege and heresy the Emperor Frederick II, who inherited from his mother, Constance, the Norman kingdom of Sicily. Frederick II, *'Stupor Mundi'*, came to be regarded by successive popes as the Antichrist, the embodiment of evil. The abasement of Frederick II, indeed the extirpation of the House of Hohenstaufen, was, in the eyes of the popes, a sacred duty, more

The Emperor Frederick II; an illustration from one of his own treatises. When Frederick's quarrel with the papacy resulted in his formal deposition in 1245, England was drawn into imperial affairs.

OVERLEAF Miniature of a friar preaching outside a church. The papacy used the newly-established orders of Dominicans and Franciscans to preach a crusade against the 'infidel' Emperor Frederick.

important than the rescue of the Holy Sepulchre from the infidel. For them, indeed, he was the infidel: his oriental harem and his sceptical, free-thinking Court at Palermo were for the popes adequate reasons to brand him as a heretic and blasphemer. But it was above all their fear of encirclement which led the popes of the thirteenth century to stop at nothing to break the Hohenstaufen power in Italy. They used every weapon in their spiritual and secular armouries; the new orders of Friars Minor and Friars Preacher (Franciscans and Dominicans) were ordered to preach a crusade against him. The popes won their great struggle with Frederick II, but it was a victory which left the papacy enfeebled and spiritually degraded. The monarch of the western Church was in those days too powerful for any single adversary and it was only Frederick's genius which delayed, for nearly thirty years, the overthrow of imperial rule in Italy. What he could not do – effectively challenge papal prerogatives – was later to be done by the monarchs of national states, notably by Philip IV, the Fair, of France.

Frederick II died in 1250, and with him fell the Holy Roman Empire, the creation of Charlemagne and of Otto the Great. In the same year St Louis of France was captured in Egypt at the disastrous Battle of Mansourah and Henry III took the cross. The year 1250 was treated by Matthew Paris as marking the end of one of history's most significant epochs. 'Many diligent investigators say that more marvels and novelties have happened during the last fifty years than in any of the similar periods preceding it. And greater things than these are to be awaited with dread in the days to come.'

'Greater things than these are to be awaited with dread'

The pious King of England and the infidel Emperor moved in quite different circles. Frederick had married in 1235, as his third wife, Henry's sister Isabella. She had a son of this marriage, Henry of Hohenstaufen, who died in 1255, thus snapping the links between the Hohenstaufen and the Plantagenets. While this link lasted, Henry, family-minded as ever, bestowed upon Frederick the affection due to a brother-in-law. Henry was by temperament a Guelf, that is a supporter of the papal cause, even if the magical influence of Frederick's personality sometimes tempted him to defy papal authority. England had, in the reign of his father John, become a fief of the papacy and Henry never seriously argued with its theocratic claims. Henry came to the throne at the end of Pope Innocent III's triumphant pontificate which marked the zenith of papal power. The bulls and decrees of the Fourth Lateran Council, held in 1215, the year before Innocent's death, went a long way towards confirming Innocent's belief in himself as the autocrat of human society, the successor to St Peter whom Christ had left 'to govern not only the universal Church but all the secular world'.

Henry III's religiosity and craven attitude to the papacy, his ambitious vanity and his love of magnificence, made him a perfect pawn for Innocent IV, that cold, crafty, Genoese canon lawyer who was willing, in the furtherance of his campaign against Frederick, to turn to secular uses the whole armoury of papal prerogatives – dispensations, excommunications, interdicts, Crusades and ecclesiastical taxation. When Frederick was alive, Innocent IV had difficulty in finding any king who would be willing to depose a legitimate fellow monarch. After his death and that of his son, Conrad IV, in 1254, things were different. Conrad had left an infant son, Conradino, and Manfred, Frederick's illegitimate son, now controlled Sicily. A contract was drawn up between Henry and the Pope, who commuted his crusading vow. Henry was to provide an army of 8,500 for the invasion of Sicily and to guarantee papal expenses to the tune of 135,541 marks. Failure to perform by the middle of 1256 would mean the placing of England under an interdict and the excommunication of the King himself. The taxes, the crusading tenths, which had been collected from the English Church to finance Henry's Crusade, were now diverted to finance the Sicilian adventure; they amounted to little more than one-third of what Henry had agreed to pay. He was well and truly the financial creature of the papacy, as pitifully in its power as had been his father John. Alas, financial worries deprived Henry of any romantic pleasure he might have got from this entanglement; he had pledged himself and his realm as sureties for the repayment of the debts of the Roman Curia.

The fear of excommunication held terrors for the pious King who attended three masses daily. Ever since his boyhood, when Pope Honororius III and the papal legate Guala helped him to keep his precarious throne, he had never wavered in filial devotion and gratitude to Rome. Now Rome was keeping her loyal son to his contract and insisting upon the punctual payment of sums which were simply unavailable. Papal envoys arrived to collect the money; they were received by Henry and Edmund, now aged twelve, who was dressed in Apulian robes. Innocent IV died in 1254 and his successor, Alexander IV, renewed the threat of interdict and excommunication against Henry. In April 1258 Henry summoned his lay and ecclesiastical magnates and told them of the Pope's terms. A few days later the leading magnates, bound together by oath, led a body of earls, barons and knights, all armed, to the palace at Westminster; leaving their swords at the door, they burst in on the King and presented to him their ultimatum. They would help raise the money to settle the Sicilian Business as long as the Pope agreed to moderate his conditions and the King to reform the state of the realm. Henry and Edward swore on the Gospels to submit themselves to the advice of the barons. In December 1258 Alexander IV issued a bull cancelling the grant of the kingdom of Sicily to Edmund; the Pope had received half the stipulated sum of 135,541 marks.

The settlement of the Sicilian Business was closely bound up with its sequel, the negotiation of a peace treaty with France, which was ratified the following year. Under it, Henry surrendered his claims to Normandy, Maine and Anjou, and acknowledged his vassal status in Gascony. The treaty marked the end of the Empire established by Henry II in the previous century and defined the frontiers of the new France. St Louis, the great European arbitrator, as his own contribution to the Sicilian question, agreed to a clause in the treaty whereby he paid for five hundred knights for two years to help papal forces fight the usurping Manfred in Sicily.

Although the Sicilian Business turned out to be a fiasco, we

OPPOSITE Thirteenth-century ivory of a bishop giving his blessing.

should not be too harsh on Henry for looking for some sort of glamorous compensation for the loss of the Angevin Empire. What appears to us to have been a lunatic entanglement had in those days many apologists. If Henry and the Pope had been more intelligent, able to command the respect of their subjects, the enterprise might have succeeded, and that beautiful and strategically vital island would have enjoyed the benefits of English rule and perhaps been spared many subsequent wars and tumults. The throne of Sicily had been offered earlier to men of greater commonsense before it was offered to Henry: to Charles of Anjou, who refused it on the instructions of his brother St Louis (later, in the 1260s, Charles became King of Sicily); and to Henry's brother, Richard of Cornwall, who said it was like being offered the moon on condition that one unhooked it from the sky.

The little-known career of Henry's brother, Richard of Cornwall, illustrates the advantages and drawbacks of being a king's younger brother. Richard probably played as great a part as anybody, apart from Henry, in Edward's life until 1272 when he died, the year Edward came to the throne. Apart from his great wealth he remains a rather shadowy figure, although we are aware of his presence at most of the important events of Henry's reign. He appears to have had much better judgment than Henry, whom he knew inside out, and was undismayed by Henry's tantrums even when directed against himself. Although Richard moved in the background of the stage, he makes a much less negative impression upon us than does that other younger brother, his nephew Edmund of Lancaster, on whose behalf his father Henry had accepted the Sicilian Crown after Richard had turned it down. This could be because Edmund was overshadowed by his strong-minded and capable elder brother Edward, whereas Henry's feebleness of character brought out Richard's positive qualities.

Henry, generous as always to his relations, gave Richard the wealthy earldom of Cornwall, to which were added the Cornish tin mines which had belonged to his mother, Isabella of

The arms of Richard of Cornwall on a shield in Westminster Abbey. The younger brother of Henry III, he was reputedly the wealthiest prince in Europe.

Angoulême. After John's death she married Hugh of Lusignan, who had been destined for her daughter, and became the mother of all those Lusignan half-brothers, who excited by their rapacity and greed the fury of the English barons. Richard married Isabella, the beautiful daughter of the elder William Marshal, first Earl of Pembroke, and the widow of Gilbert de Clare, Earl of Gloucester. This marriage brought Richard into close association with the baronial leaders, to whose grievances about Henry's failings he listened sympathetically. Henry kept him loyal by plying him with grants of land: he gave him, for example, a large part of southern Wales, which had belonged to the de Braose family. Richard played an active part in promoting the marriage of his sister Isabella to the Emperor Frederick II.

On many occasions Richard attacked the King for his greed and his maladministration. In 1238 he was the mouthpiece of the baronial opposition to Simon de Montfort's 'shot-gun' marriage to his and the King's sister, Eleanor. Richard's wife Isabella was the sister of Eleanor's previous husband, William Marshal the younger, and Eleanor had taken an oath of chastity after his death in the presence of the Archbishop of Canterbury. As Matthew Paris recorded:

> The realm was vehemently disturbed because, against the wishes of his magnates and in particular of Earl Richard, and in disregard of St Edmund's advice, the King arranged the marriage between Eleanor and Simon. Also, he tried to do other important things although he had promised his magnates not to act without them. In the end, however, Earl Richard, the spokesman of all the rest, was pacified.

Richard was 'pacified' by fresh grants from his brother, which included the forest of Dartmoor. He was quickly reconciled to Henry and Simon, much to the dismay of the barons.

After his wife's death in childbirth in 1240 Richard went to live abroad, saying that he could no longer endure the desolation of England, a feeling which would be echoed by many Englishmen today. The birth of Edward the previous year deprived him of some of his expectations and weakened his close connection with the English baronage. As the only brother of a childless king he had contemplated pressing his right to Gascony and Poitou, and had considered claiming a special position in England as the country's biggest landowner. Instead he contented himself with a rather different role – that of a very influential figure in the diplomatic world. He used his good offices when they were needed, mediating between Frederick II and Gregory IX, negotiating with the Sultan of Egypt for the release of Simon's brother, Amauri de Montfort, and other French prisoners. Wherever he went, he was received with great honour.

He took as his second wife, Sanchia, the daughter of Raymond-Berengar of Provence and sister of the Queens of France and England. This second marriage, unlike the first, bound him closely to the Court and the unpopular Savoyards and other foreign influences. Richard became the political ally of his brother and left the way clear for the rise of Simon de Montfort. He stood loyally by Henry and Edward during the critical years to come, never forgetting to further his own business interests. He financed the operations needed to reform the coinage and Henry mortgaged to him all the Jews in the country. He lent Henry money for the building schemes so close to his heart, and he lent the young Edward 4,000 marks to subdue his rebellious Welsh subjects.

The richest man in Europe

Richard, although reputedly the richest man in Europe, evidently did not find the amassing of wealth and secondary titles a sufficient compensation for the lack of a throne. He had, it is true, the commonsense to refuse the Pope's offer of the Sicilian Crown, but that of the Holy Roman Empire was a different matter. Such was the mystique of the title, carrying with it the chance of being crowned Emperor by the Pope in Rome and the theoretical claim of universal secular suzerainty, that the most realistic and intelligent of men found it a prize hard to resist if dangled before their eyes.

In 1250, the year of Frederick's death, started the Great Interregnum in Germany. It had really begun four years earlier when Innocent IV deposed and banned Frederick II for sacrilege and heresy at the General Council at Lyons. This led at once to civil war in Germany and to the election of two anti-Caesars, both of whom died shortly afterwards. With the death of Frederick, Germany no longer had even a titular king and the country sank further into anarchy, at the mercy of robber barons great and small. The electors preferred to have as King of the Romans somebody with no power in Germany: history had shown that a powerful and able king, backed by his own towns, castles and territories inside Germany, could effectively impose imperial power over many of the dukes, princes and lesser nobility. Thus it came about that they chose Richard to be King of the Romans in 1257. He was the only Englishman who ever attempted to rule the Holy Roman Empire. All the Germans liked about him was his money, but even that ran out in the end. He distributed it prodigally amongst his Rhineland vassals but he never succeeded in making his presence felt inside Germany.

The Common Enterprise

The conclusion of the Sicilian Business in 1258 was the immediate cause of the Provisions of Oxford in the same year, one of the most important events in the history of the English constitution. From that date onwards, until the death of Henry, the barons, and then Edward, were in control. As we have seen the helpless Henry, bankrupt and threatened with excommunication, had turned to the barons. The baronial leaders, Simon de Montfort, Earl Richard of Gloucester, Peter of Savoy and Hugh Bigod, brother of the Earl of Norfolk, drove a hard bargain in return for getting Henry off the Sicilian hook. He had to consent to the reform of the realm by a committee of twenty-four, twelve nominated by Henry and twelve by the barons. The barons claimed to be choosing their members as representatives, not simply of the magnates, but of the community as a whole – *'ex parte communitatis'*. The baronial movement of 1258–62 became known, in Simon de Montfort's words, as *'la comune emprise'* – the Common Enterprise. The Great Council of magnates was no longer a consultative body; it had been forced, in consequence of Henry's incapacity and against its own

The Provisions of Oxford

Early in 1258 a number of the leading magnates forced Henry to agree to the appointment of a committee of twenty-four, twelve to be elected by them and twelve by the King, which would recommend measures for the reform of the kingdom. Their proposals, contained in the Provisions of Oxford, included the setting up of a council of fifteen magnates to advise the King, oversee Chancery and the Exchequer, and control all wardships and lands which fell into the King's hands. For two years Henry was under the tutelage of the barons until, in 1260, the settlement began to break down. After Henry had been released from his commitment by St Louis' decision at Amiens in 1264, civil war broke out.

OPPOSITE Part of the text of the Provisions of Oxford. Amongst the signatures on the bottom right of the page are those of the Earls of Leicester, Valence, Warwick and Gloucester.

RIGHT The emblem of Simon de Montfort, a silver fork-tailed lion, displayed on a decorative shield in Westminster Abbey. Simon played a prominent part in the baronial revolt from the beginning, but it was not until 1263 that he became its undisputed leader.

BELOW A king followed by clergy and barons, the two sections of society from which he traditionally chose his advisers to form the King's Council.

signaturi thesauros suos in locis diversis religiosis. Postea autem dominus Edwardus cum magna difficultate ad hoc inductus se supposuit statutorum ordinationi et provisioni. Cum eodem consenserunt et ex tunc sui consiliarii facti, scilicet domini Johannes de Baillol, Johannes de Gray, Stephanus Lungespeye et Willelmus de Monte Alto. In brevi vero providebant de statu hospicii regni et hospicii domini Regis. Rogatum autem erat dominus Rex quod ultra maneret cum eo justitia Angliae et alia exire. Magnates et ceteri barones providendas quae non possunt cito ut de facili consuetudini et effectui mancipari. Providebant etiam in brevi unde cum domino Rege apud London plures conjugerent alienigenas tam Romanos quam mercatores Caursinos et alios. Ad depositionem etiam et punitionem clericorum tunc posuerunt barones praesentes et eadem confederata fuit cum monachis scilicet Warham procedit barones in agendis suis ut verum bonum suae sententiae.

Fuerunt etiam in eodem parliamento apud Oxon. xxiiij. electi, videlicet xij. ex parte domini Regis et totidem ex parte comitum, quorum ordinationibus et provisionibus dominus Rex et dominus Edwardus filius ejus se supposuerunt super statu eodem et toto regni Angliae correctione et in melius reformatione. Aliqua etiam fuerunt ibidem et alibi provisa quae inferius continentur. Provisio facta apud Oxon.

Provisum est quod de quolibet comitatu eligantur quatuor discreti et legales milites qui quolibet die ubi tenetur comitatus conveniant ad audiendum omnes querelas de quibuscumque transgressionibus et injuriis quibuscumque personis illatis per vicecomites, ballivos seu quoscumque alios, et ad faciendum attachiamenta quae ad dictas querelas pertinent usque ad primum adventum capitalis justiciarii in partes illas, ita quod sufficientes capiant plegios a conquerente de prosequendo et similiter ab eo de quo queritur veniendi et jus recipiendi coram praefato justiciario in primo adventu suo. Et quod praedicti quatuor milites irrotulari faciant omnes praedictas querelas cum suis attachiamentis ordinate et serie, scilicet de quolibet hundredo separatim et per se, ita quod praefatus justiciarius in primo adventu suo possit audire et terminare praefatas querelas singillatim de quolibet hundredo. Et scire faciant vicecomiti quod venire faciat coram praefato justiciario in primo adventu suo ad dies et loca quae eis scire faciet omnes hundredarios et ballivos suos, ita quod quilibet hundredarius venire faciat omnes conquerentes et defendentes de ballia sua successive secundum quod praefatus justiciarius duxerit de praedicto hundredo placitare. Et tot et tales tam milites quam alios liberos et legales homines de ballia sua per quos rei veritas melius convinci poterit, ita quod omnes simul et semel non vexentur, set tot veniant quot possint venire de placitis et terminari.

Et provisum est quod nullus miles de praedictis comitatibus occasione hujus provisionis quod non ponatur in juratis vel assisis per cartam domini Regis defendatur nec quietus sit quo ad provisionem istam sic factam pro communi utilitate totius regni.

Electi ex parte domini Regis.

Dominus London. episcopus.
D. W. electus Wint.
D. H. filius Regis Alemanniae.
D. J. comes Warenn.
D. Guido de Lysinnia.
D. W. de Valence.
D. J. comes Warewic.
D. Johannes Mansell.
Frater J. de Derlington.
Abbas Westmon.
D. H. de Wengham.

Electi ex parte comitum et baronum.

Dominus Wigorn. episcopus.
D. Simon comes Leycestriae.
D. Ric. comes Glovernie.
D. Hunfrid comes Hereford.
D. Rogerus Marescall.
D. Rogerus de Mortuo Mari.
D. J. filius Galfridi.
D. Hugo le Bygot.
D. Ric. de Gray.
D. W. Bardulf.
D. P. de Monte Forti.
D. Hugo Dispensarius.

inclinations, to assume the functions of the King's Council. The barons were aware of the novelty and significance of what they were doing; they were denying to the King the freedom of appointing whom he wished to be members of his own Council. They wrote to the Pope telling him of the dramatic new state of affairs, 'for there has been a new and sudden change'.

The man, more than any other, who is thought to have been behind this 'new and sudden change', was Simon de Montfort, Earl of Leicester. Simon is one of history's controversial characters; to his admirers he is an enlightened liberal reformer, anxious for the middle classes to have their say in the running of the country, and to his enemies he is an unscrupulous megalomaniac, prepared to stop at nothing to overthrow the King and the established government and to seize power for himself. He was at least a man who aroused strong emotions. The turmoil and confusion of the years 1258–67, the period of the baronial movement, is dramatised by the relationship of the mighty Earl of Leicester with his young admirer, adversary and nephew, the Lord Edward.

Simon de Montfort came from an old and impoverished family in the Ile de France. Only ruins now remain of the family stronghold of Montfort-l'Amaury, about thirty miles south-west of Paris on the edge of the Forest of Rambouillet. His father, the Count of Toulouse, was the austere and fanatical leader of the Albigensian Crusades and Simon was his second son, born around 1208. He inherited his father's deep religious faith, military ability and enormous ambition. The family connections with England arose from the marriage of Simon's grandfather to a sister of the Earl of Leicester, a great landowner in England and Normandy. When, in 1204, the Earl of Leicester died leaving no direct heirs, his English lands were divided between his two sisters, Amicia, the mother of Simon's crusading father, and Margaret, wife of the Earl of Winchester. Simon, the younger son of a younger son, was to struggle pertinaciously and successfully to obtain for himself the earldom of Leicester, with which went the Stewardship of

OPPOSITE A fourteenth-century map showing England, Scotland and Wales.

Ros
Catenes
ciuitas S. Andree
Estrivelin
SCOCIA
Clud
Glasgu
Galeweia
Tued
Rokesburc
Laudiana
Berewic
Roket
Thine
Dunelm
Carleolii
Furneis
Ebor
Heudernesse 7 Ridale
Hul
Beverle
Bridlington
Leicestr
Stanford
Norhamton
WALLIA
Hereford
Wirecestre
Gloucestria
Snaudun
Bangor
Bris
tol
London
Roffa
Medewei
Deuonia
Colecestr

England and many large estates. The landless, penniless and ambitious young adventurer was determined to establish himself quickly in the feudal world. There were, he decided, two ways of doing this: to claim the Leicester lands and to make a rich marriage, both of which objects were best pursued at the Francophile court of young Henry III.

To London Simon therefore went in 1230 and, before long, he had struck up an intimate friendship with Henry. Like most friendships of that frivolous and impulsive King, it was by its nature ephemeral. However, in its heady early days it bought Simon great rewards. He secured his earldom, thus becoming one of the great magnates of England. The office of Steward of England, which originally designated the person who should bring the king his food and drink at ceremonial feasts, had gathered up over the years many wide and vague claims, which Simon could expect to use to further his power and influence in the land.

Secure in his earldom and in the King's favour, Simon's next task was to marry a rich wife. Whom should he marry but the King's sister Eleanor, widow of the Earl of Pembroke? Marriages of royal princesses were in those days important acts of State and they were preceded by months of consultation between the king and baronial advisors before the final decision was made. This had happened before Eleanor's first marriage in 1224 to William Marshal the younger, Earl of Pembroke, when Henry was still a boy. The Earl was one of the most powerful men in England and the magnates had wanted to secure his loyalty to the young King. Now Henry married off his sister to Simon in haste and secrecy, thus presenting the barons with a *fait accompli*. It was, ironically, arbitrary behaviour of this sort on the King's part and the conviction that he was incapable of governing responsibly which later led Simon to take up arms against him. Simon's marriage set the pattern for the barons' future discontents; in their eyes Simon was one of those hateful upstart foreigners who, together with Henry's Poitevin half-brothers and the Queen's rapacious Provençal and Savoyard relations, were out to enrich themselves and impoverish the

The official seal of Simon de Montfort showing him hunting.

country. In the case of Simon they were partly right. Although he and his wife between them owned a large part of England – most of East Anglia, the home and southern counties – they were not satisfied; both enjoyed the pedantic assertion of obscure and disputed property rights and both reproached Henry ceaselessly that he had not given his sister a larger marriage-portion.

Simon's period of favour with Henry came to a sudden end immediately after Edward's birth in June 1239. The King publicly insulted Simon at the Queen's churching in Westminster Abbey; he accused him, amongst other things, of having seduced his sister before their marriage, this being the real reason for its undue haste. From then onwards Henry had a love-hate attitude to Simon: he feared him and he used him; outbursts of rage were followed by acts of reconciliation. Simon despised the King, but remained a loyal and useful servant, accepting commissions great and small, in Gascony and elsewhere.

Simon's gradual transition from opposition to rebellion against the King falls into three phases – the swearing of the Provisions of Oxford by Henry, Edward and the barons in 1258; the King's repudiation of them in 1260–1; and the Mise or Award of Amiens of January 1264, when St Louis, having been asked to arbitrate between the King and the barons, pronounced against the Provisions. It is now thought that Simon did not play a very prominent part in the events which led up to that day in 1258 when the chief magnates and their followers burst in on Henry in his palace at Westminster. However, being intelligent, idealistic and clear-sighted, Simon must have watched Henry's misuse of government with growing exasperation. As a Frenchman, he could compare the wisdom and ability of St Louis, that most perfect monarch of his age, with the inadequacies of his brother-in-law. As a foreigner in England, he saw more clearly than could most Englishmen what should be done to put things right.

Henry's reign was a great period in English history. Not only did it produce great men of varied attainments like Roger Bacon, Robert Grosseteste, Matthew Paris, Henry de Bracton and Simon himself, but it also saw the expansion and development of common law and legal theory and the steady growth of royal power. Never before had the Crown wielded such power and never had the reality of royal authority been brought so closely home to subjects of all classes. Henry's crime was the perversion of the uses of royal power. He lost the respect of the barons; by excluding them from his counsels, by relying instead on toadying officials and the insolent Poitevins, he exasperated their sense of injustice. To this was to be added his conduct of foreign and military affairs; he had tried three times to recover lost lands in France; Llewelyn in Wales was ravaging the Marches and planning an alliance with Scotland. Each of Henry's ventures meant more disgrace and heavier debts.

Until 1258 the barons had had no wish to control the government, but simply to be consulted. All they wanted was that England be governed under the existing system, without incessant demands for aid and subsidies and without repeated military fiascos. Once, however, they had been provoked to take power out of Henry's control, they found that the people had many justifiable grievances, which they set out to redress.

We do not know much about young Edward's activities at this time. He appears to have spent most of the period between his return from Gascony and his reluctant affirmation by oath of the Provisions of Oxford in chivalrous exercises and in the neglect of those estates which his father had quixotically bestowed upon him. His campaigning in Wales was a failure; he

Initial portrait of Robert Grosseteste, Bishop of Lincoln from 1235 to 1253. A scholar and reformer, he had a great and beneficial influence on the development of the medieval church.

was as yet no match for Llewelyn, with whom a truce was made in 1259. Edward's first real appearance in the drama of King versus barons was in 1260 when he was temporarily swayed by Simon's personality and arguments and, for the first and last time in his life, was tempted to side with Simon against his father. Who can be surprised that Edward at the age of twenty-one should have been attracted by the great Earl? Simon was one of the most impressive knights of his age, of captivating personality, internationally recognised as a powerful and important figure. This man of influence was also a friend of saintly men and scholars. To his political ruthlessness and

stubbornness was joined strong Christian piety, idealism and sympathy for the unprivileged and the oppressed. He sought the company of men like the Franciscan Adam March and the scholar-saint Robert Grosseteste, Bishop of Lincoln, and he derived spiritual nourishment from his proximity to them. The compassionate Simon, the hater of arbitrary tyranny and oppression, found his reward after his death when the wandering friars in their sermons spoke of him as a saint and martyr, as the saviour of the poor.

In 1260 Simon hoped to enter into an alliance with his nephew Edward. He suspected, rightly, that the King would

Henry III and Queen Eleanor returning from Gascony in 1260. While Henry was in France he heard rumours of his son's disloyalty, so hurriedly returned home to confront him.

repudiate the Provisions as soon as he dared; Henry was, in fact, waiting for a papal dispensation from his oath and for baronial solidarity to weaken. February of that year was a month of acute crisis both for Edward and for Simon. Henry was in France and Simon was determined to hold a parliament in his absence; the Provisions prescribed three annual parliaments at Candlemas, in June and in October. He won Edward's support for this revolutionary scheme. Henry in France learned with horror of his son's disloyalty and returned hurriedly to England. Simon was accused of *lèse-majesté*, and Edward submitted himself and his cause to the judgment of his father and uncle, Richard of Cornwall. Thus ended the brief alliance of Simon and Edward, whose 'defection' made him Simon's greatest enemy. The years 1260–5 tell the story of Edward versus Simon and the barons.

Simon disliked the people whose rights he was asserting. After St Louis' judgment against the Provisions, he was in two minds whether to stay in England: 'I have seen many peoples and countries, Christian and pagan, but never have I seen a nation so fickle and false as the people of England.' He had more reason to be disillusioned by the betrayals of his fellow barons than by the fickleness of the people. Edward as a military opponent behaved in many instances with English 'falseness and fickleness'. The author of *The Song of Lewes*, a long Latin poem presenting the barons' constitutional arguments, wrote, 'he was a lion for pride and ferocity, but a pard for inconstancy and changeableness, not keeping his word or promise, but excusing himself with fair words'. One of his first acts after the civil war had started was to break a truce with Simon's son, Henry de Montfort, at Gloucester.

After the Mise of Amiens, Simon had two alternatives – to accept the award and abandon the Provisions or to fight to uphold his own particular ideal of royal government. He chose, as we know, the latter. St Louis could hardly have declared for the diminution of an anointed king's freedom in choosing his ministers or exercising legal authority. He was expressing in his judgment the opinions of the age. It has been said of Simon by certain historians that he set himself up against the whole theory of royal authority in the west, the only example of collective government by vassals being in Jerusalem and the Latin states of the east. Simon was in a greater dilemma than that other great rebel four hundred years later, Oliver Cromwell. He was a royalist and his political thought was impregnated by ideas of the rights and duties of kingship. He would never have wanted to be a dictator, whatever is asserted to the contrary. The same was true of the other barons, who supported his cause – their fundamental royalism shook the constancy of their resolve and put them at a disadvantage even with a weak king.

In any event, the Mise of Amiens resulted in civil war and this gave Edward his chance to turn from jousting to more dangerous sports. The supreme moment of the war for Simon was the Battle of Lewes in May 1264. Simon and his adherents – barons, knights, bowmen, bishops, friars and Londoners – gathered together in the Forest of the Weald, a few miles north of Lewes, inspired and united by a belief in their high cause.

Kenilworth Castle in Warwickshire, the home of Simon de Montfort. The twelfth-century keep which he used is on the right. The ruined hall on the left dates from the fourteenth century.

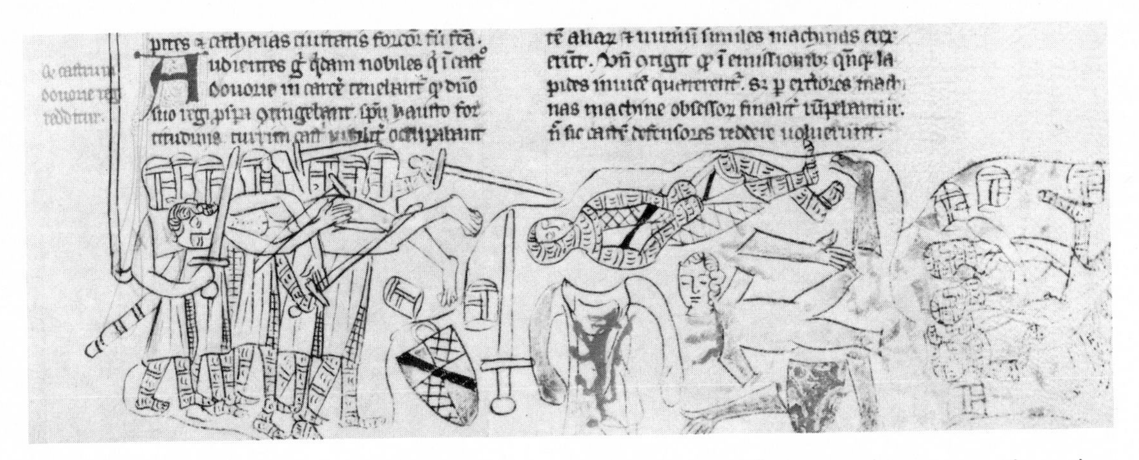

The death of Simon de Montfort at the Battle of Evesham and the subsequent decapitation and mutilation of his body.

Until the battle started Simon made peace overtures, reiterating his unswerving fidelity to Henry and claiming that he only wished to overthrow the King's real enemies. Edward's reply to this overture was that the barons were 'perfidious traitors'. Simon's troops wore the white cross of the Crusaders over their armour, as if to emphasise the sacred nature of their cause.

Simon won at Lewes a great and near-bloodless victory; only a few knights were killed, the dead being mostly men-at-arms and Londoners. The reason for the high mortality among the Londoners was that Edward hunted them down in retribution for their insulting treatment of his mother – they had attacked her barge as she was leaving the Tower of London for Windsor. He pursued them over hill and dale, slaughtering several hundred of them; he was so carried away by his avenging zeal that, when he returned to the fray, the battle was over and his father a prisoner.

After Lewes, Simon was in charge, and for fifteen months he ruled the country. The battle over, Henry delivered Edward as hostage for his renewed promise to observe the Provisions. At the beginning of 1265, Simon summoned what is sometimes called the Great Parliament, to distinguish it from the Model Parliament of Edward I. For the first time in history, the cities and boroughs sent representatives, as did also the rural nobility. Edward was theoretically released from custody after swearing to recognise the new ordinances; in fact, he was still kept under strict supervision. His one thought was to escape, mobilise the royalists and crush his rebellious uncle and godfather by force of arms. His chance came one day in March 1265 when he was hunting near Hereford; as planned with friends in advance, he drew ahead of his keeper in pursuit of a deer and then made a dash for it. He was free!

Edward next day joined Gilbert de Clare, Earl of Gloucester, at Ludlow. Gilbert had been Simon's colleague from the very beginning of the civil war; he had fought with him at Lewes and been a member of the triumvirate which afterwards ruled the country. Gilbert's defection was not due to any disagreement with Simon about principle, but to his disapproval of what he considered to be his overweaning ambition for himself and his family. As the price for his help he made Edward swear to maintain the good charters and customs, to expel aliens and to admit only Englishmen to the Council.

With the vigorous Edward free once more, optimism returned to the royalist camp. The end was to come quickly for Simon. On 4 August 1265 he was out-manoeuvred and encircled by the troops of Edward and Gloucester at Evesham. He only had a handful of men and he knew, as he saw Edward's troops closing in on him, that there was no way out: 'Let us commend our souls to God, because our bodies are theirs.' He was impressed by the professional disposition of Edward's troops: 'By the arm of St James [his favourite oath], they are approaching wisely; they learned this from me.' The battle was short and savage. Simon fell and his body was horribly mutilated; his head and limbs were hacked off and the trunk thrown to the dogs.

Simon, the victim of Evesham, entered the hearts and minds of the common people; soon it was being reported that miracles had been performed on the spot where his body had been so unceremoniously treated. Edward, who admired and then destroyed Simon, was later to have a government which combined traditional, legitimate authority with the statesmanship of Simon. In Edward I, wrote Winston Churchill, 'the great earl had found his true heir. The victor of Evesham was the true pupil of the vanquished.'

3
Crusader and King 1265–74

AFTER THE BATTLE of Evesham, royal power once again ruled the land. It was some time before all resistance was overcome: London was still in the hands of the baronial party; Simon's impregnable castle of Kenilworth was to hold out for over a year afterwards; and Simon's widow, the Countess of Leicester, was defending Dover Castle. It is reassuring to know that Edward was relatively magnanimous in his treatment of former opponents. By 1267 the realm had been pacified. Edward, aged twenty-eight, had emerged triumphantly from a tough apprenticeship in kingcraft. He had played the leading role in saving royal authority by destroying the combination of forces which had usurped the King's functions, and he had brought the rebellion to an end.

Edward was not yet absorbed in the creation of a unified kingdom at home, and his instincts were, now that peace prevailed once again in his own country, to seek the company of his royal uncles and cousins on the Continent. A glance at some genealogical tables will show that western Europe was at this time a group of large estates whose owners were all closely related. Their frequent arguments about territorial rights, leading sometimes to sanguinary wars, partook more of the nature of family than national quarrels. Edward was as much at home on the Continent as in England. The Emperor Frederick II Hohenstaufen had married his aunt, Isabella; his father, St Louis, Charles of Anjou and his uncle, Richard of Cornwall, King of the Romans, had married the Provençal sisters; his brother-in-law was Alfonso X, the King of Castile; and there were dozens of other smaller matrimonial alliances which brought principalities and duchies into this vast family network.

The Lord Edward, now nearly thirty, was one of the great figures on the European scene, enjoying universal esteem and admiration. In the eyes of his relations on the Continent he was king in all but name. The occasional instance of deviousness and brutality mars the picture of this young prince, otherwise replete with knightly virtues. His followers and retainers had a reputation for violence; there were stories that they despoiled

PREVIOUS PAGES A naval battle from the earliest known French translation of Vegetius' *De re militari*, 1270. This treatise, written in the fourth century AD, became the military bible of Europe for many centuries.

OPPOSITE The Lord Edward and some young nobles being instructed in the arts of warfare from *De re militari*.

Venez amoy seus chevalers q volez aver honur de chevalerie

OPPOSITE St Louis in scenes demonstrating his piety including bathing the feet of the poor, from *Le Livre des Faiz Monseigneur St Louis.*

priories and ill-treated monks, and Edward was said to have horribly mutilated a young man who had in some way displeased him. These should perhaps be looked at as examples of the arrogance and impetuosity of a young nobleman used to having his own way. He was indeed hasty and quick to take offence, and although, towards the end of his life he could be harsh and stern, he was seldom wantonly cruel.

Edward turned his thoughts in the direction of a Crusade. In June 1268, he and some of his friends took the cross at Northampton from the papal legate, Ottobuono Fieschi, who was preaching a Crusade on the Pope's instructions. Cardinal Ottobuono had been entrusted by Clement IV with the difficult task of helping Henry III and Edward restore peace and order in their troubled country. From 1265 to 1268 he was the dominant influence in the English government. With his able colleague, Tedaldo Visconti, shortly to become Pope Gregory X, he worked efficiently and harmoniously with Henry and Edward, and in an astonishingly short time the wounds created by royalist and rebel barons and bishops, knights and burghers were healed. This exercise in social and political reconciliation is sometimes given as a rare example of perfect co-operation between Church and State, the joint recognition of the underlying unity of western Christendom.

Now, signed with the cross, Edward prepared to go on Crusade. He left Dover with Eleanor, his faithful camp-follower, in August 1270, intending to join his uncle, St Louis, at Aigues Mortes in Provence, whither they would proceed to Africa and do battle with the formidable Baibars (or Bibars), Sultan of Egypt, who now ruled Palestine. On the way they planned to visit Tunis, whose Moslem Emir was, in St Louis' eyes, ready for conversion to Christianity.

St Louis was the most attractive figure of the thirteenth century and the best ruler. He was a year or two younger than his brother-in-law Henry; they both inherited their thrones when under age, and both had the inevitable difficulties with rebellious and powerful vassals. Louis' subjects had not reckoned on the strength of his formidable mother, Blanche of

de la bonne royne et dudit
roy son filz furent mandez
gens darmes de toutes pars
qui sassemblerent tous en j.
iour ordonne et estably au
boys de vincennes dont ledit
conte de champaigne fut
fort esbahy. et congnoissat
sa faulte et aussi quil ne
povoit resister envoya dili
gemment devers ledit glorieux
roy de ses plus privez et fea
bles serviteurs luy supplier et
requerir quil luy voulsist
pardonner loffense et appai
ser la fureur quil avoit con
tre luy offrant luy donner a
heritaige monsteriau ou
fourt yonne et bray sur
seine. Et ses messages reto
nez devers luy qui navoiet
rien peu conclurre Ledit cote
y vint en personne et cria lors
mercy au roy en toute humi
lite et luy demanda pardon.
Et a la fin fist tant par le
moyen de laditte royne mere
du glorieux saint loys que
le roy luy pardonna. et luy
demourerent lesdiz monste
reau et bray sur seine qui
furent venz a son demaine

De la maniere de vivre du
glorieux saint loys. et comt
le roy des assassins le voulut
faire empoysonner. viij.e C.
En lan mil cc.
xxxvj. ledit glori
eux saint loys co
menca a vivre tres austeremt
et a son retour doultre mer
encores continua de mener
vie plus estroitte. car par
aucun temps il destoit la
haire principalement chun
vendredi de karesme de ladvet
et des quatre festes nredame
Contraingnoit son corps p
ieusne et rigoreuse affliction
a servir a lesperit. Souvent
oyoit sermons et predicatios
et tresvoulentiers y faisoit
estre ses enfans auaines
lors quant on lisoit aucune

St Louis arriving in Damietta in Egypt on his first Crusade to win back Jerusalem from the infidel.

Castile, nor on the irresistible saintliness of her son. He turned out to be shrewd, active and practical, as well as saintly, and under his rule France became the most powerful and respected country in Europe. Henry was extraordinarily lucky to have in St Louis a brother-in-law who did not exploit his follies and incompetence. Henry gave him ample provocation: in 1242 he came to the aid of his step-father, Hugh of Lusignan, who was leading a last ditch rebellion against St Louis in Poitou, which King John had lost to Louis VIII and which Henry longed to recover. After defeating Henry soundly at Taillebourg, St Louis treated him magnanimously, unnecessarily so in the eyes of most French historians.

Edward and St Louis would have made good partners in this Eighth (and last) Crusade. Both men owed their influence and success to the fact that they were completely at home in their times. Both were devoutly orthodox, hating heresy and accepting the traditional primacy of the papacy. Both were thought to be just and impartial. Although one was a saint and the other a sinner, their similarities of character stand out when compared, for example, with that of Edward's other uncle by marriage, the papal *bête noire*, Frederick II.

Edward and St Louis were the last crusaders in the medieval tradition. By the end of the thirteenth century, the crusading ideal was losing its strength. There were many reasons for this, but the perversion of the conception of a Holy War by both popes and kings was probably the main one. The popes had, as we have seen, in their desire to retain and to expand their Italian territorial possessions, turned the overthrowing of their arch enemy, Frederick II, into a sacred cause. This misuse of the crusading ideal for selfish political purposes on the part of the popes had shocked and disillusioned rulers and their subjects. One of the leading sceptics was the brother of St Louis, Charles of Anjou, now King of Sicily. He was indeed planning a 'crusade' – not against the Sultan of Egypt but against the Byzantine Christian Emperor at Constantinople.

Ever since Pope Urban II announced the First Crusade at Clermont in November 1095, the idea of the recovery of the Holy Land had pervaded men's minds. 'If I forget thee, O Jerusalem, may my right hand forget her cunning.' What had until then been a pilgrim's progress to Jerusalem was turned into a Holy War. Great had been the fervour of all classes after Urban II had made his famous speech, frequently interrupted by cries of '*Deus le vult*' ('God wills it'). This was the response of the west to the appeal of the Byzantine Emperor, Alexius Comnenus, for help against the infidel.

Two centuries later, Jerusalem was again in the hands of the infidel. It had twice been recovered, only to be lost again. The Crusades were a history of heroism, treachery, brutality, stupidity and, above all, faith. In spite of the odds against them, the crusaders had founded the various Latin kingdoms of Outremer and held on to them, with varying degrees of success, against the assaults of Arabs, Mongols and Turks.

St Louis' first Crusade (1249–54) was made to win back Jerusalem after it had been sacked and captured by the Turks. Although his campaign was a disastrous failure, he was not in the least discouraged and it remained his chief aim to lead another Crusade. The occasion came with the military successes of Baibars in Syria and the Holy Land. He had captured Caesarea and Haifa, and was threatening the last Christian strongholds of Antioch and Acre.

Baibars (his full name was Ruku ad-Din Baibars Bundukdari) rose from being a Mongolian slave to a second Saladin. He was a Mameluk (or Mamluk) from south Russia, and had been

OVERLEAF
A map of the Middle East from Torsellus' *Handbook for Crusaders*. Above, Mesopotamia, Babylon and the rivers Euphrates and Tigris can be clearly identified. On the right is Egypt, with two pyramids, three abbey churches and an irrigation scheme on the Nile. In the centre, the coast of Palestine; among the towns named are Byblos, Tyre, Sidon and Caesarea. To the left is the coast of Asia Minor and the island of Cyprus.

Partia extendit ulŕ tygrim usq ad indum fluuium ubi india terminat(ur) et claudit intra se asynam.

Tygris

Me so po ta mi a syri e

Per sia

Rages

Eufrates

Cal dea

babiloia.

Cele syria

Alia syria que arabia

syria ta masci

syria

a syria que galilea que dicitur caput magis esdrelo

syria palestine

syria palestine

phylistym

Culfum caramele

Mons cruo

Laiacium.

Port(us) palon

Malmistra.

Malo

Adena

Tersum

Lamum

Port(us) lobliga

Curtum

Janigum

Salefium

Lena de labugara

Portus pini

Scolius pruualun

Port(us) caualerius

Papatolla

Portus palopoli

Crionarium

Spune

Insula de oliuis

Scopuu

Dragantu

Stallimine

Calad

Castru lobadu

Castelorizi

Sci nicolai

Sci gregorii

Satalia uet(us)

Satalia

agiospendi

Aratia

port(us) Jauethu

silitonie

finiga

Solorn. Polsin. Gliata. Liga. Lena. valania. Margath. Tortosa. Tripolis. Nephym. Botrum. Biblium. Beritum. Sydon. Tyrus. Scandalii. Casale lapti. Acon. Cayfas. Castru p(er)egrinor(um). Cesarea. Arsur. Jopen.

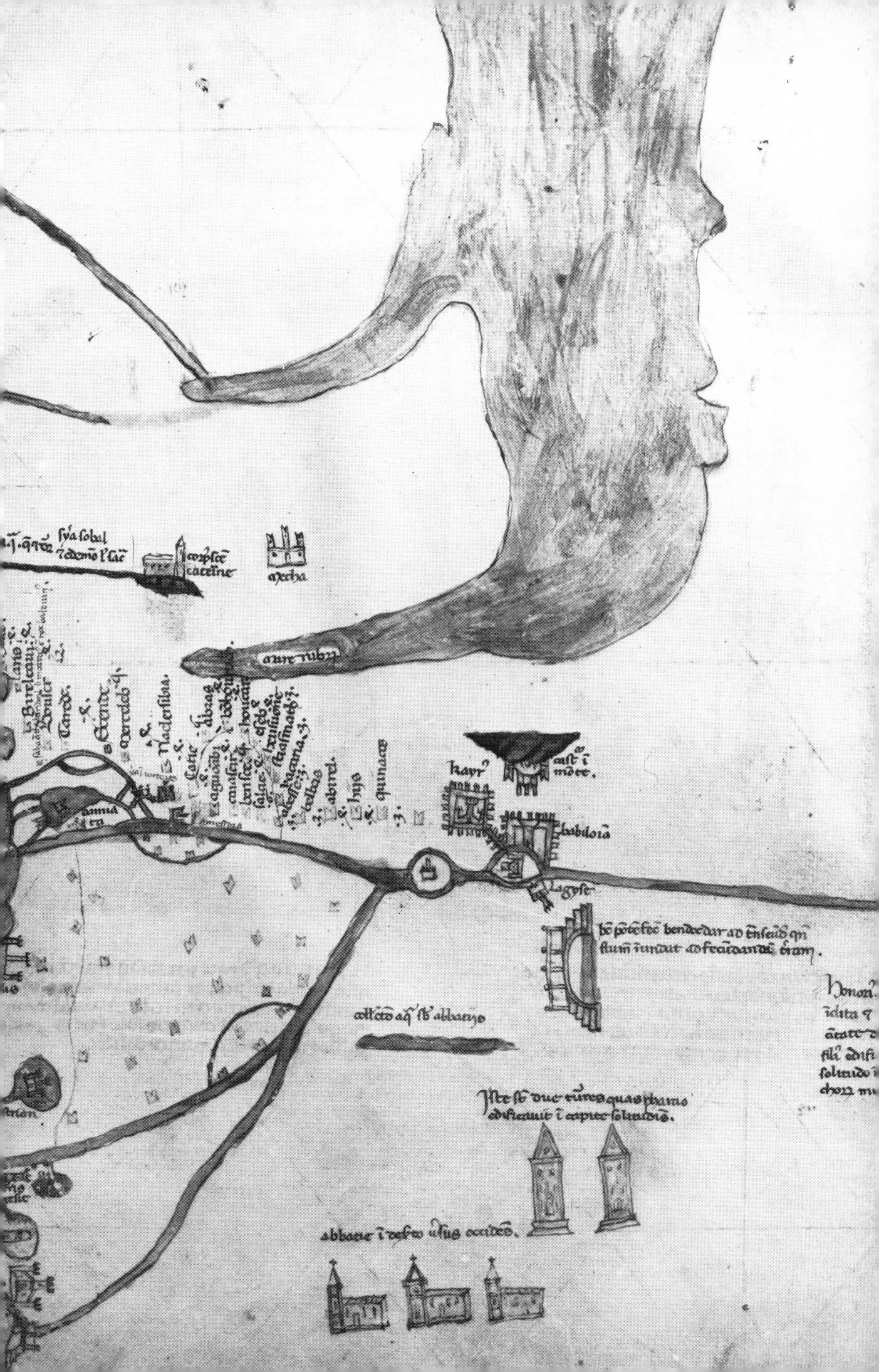

bought in the Cairo marketplace for the Sultan's Mameluk Guard. In 1260, while they were out hunting, he stabbed the Sultan in the back and promptly had himself declared Sultan of Egypt. A fanatical Moslem, he set himself the task of extinguishing the crusading kingdoms. Baibars (meaning 'the panther') was a huge man with brown skin, blue eyes and a resonant voice. In audacity, tenacity and religiosity, there was no one, Christian or infidel, to compare with him. He destroyed one Christian castle after another, the Templars and Hospitallers putting up a heroic but vain resistance. Great was the gloom among the faithful: Christ, they said, was enjoying the humiliation of the Christians. By capturing the fortress of Safed, Baibars gained control of Galilee; in 1268 Antioch fell and with it the first Frankish state in Outremer collapsed. 'Franks' was the name given by infidels and eastern Christians alike to the Crusaders from the west.

Horrified by Baibars' conquests, St Louis took the cross for the second time in 1267. Henry III talked of going with him but never really intended to: it was to be Edward's Crusade, not his. The country responded enthusiastically; there was a general desire to forget the immediate past and to expiate the recent civil strife by an attack on the enemy of Christendom. It was agreed at the Hoketide Parliament of April 1270 that there should be a general levy of one-twentieth of every citizen's goods and chattels. This was an unprecedented step: previous Crusades had been financed by papal taxation of the clergy, but now barons, prelates and freemen were all participating. By these means £30,000 were raised. In addition, St Louis advanced 70,000 livres for Edward's expenses on the security of the customs and excise of Bordeaux; the collection of these taxes was farmed out to the Italian merchant bankers. The cost of Edward's holy enterprise, which was three times as great as that of Henry's reconstruction of Westminster Abbey, was borne by the Jews, the merchant bankers, the levy of English goods and chattels, and by taxes on the Gascon vineyards.

When Edward arrived at Aigues Mortes in August, he found that St Louis had just left for Tunis. He had set sail on 1 July at the head of a formidable expedition. With him were his three surviving sons and the flower of the French nobility, many of them the sons of comrades on his earlier Crusade. The Emir of Tunis, however, far from being ready for conversion, was preparing to defend his capital at Carthage. Louis arrived on 18 July in the full heat of the African summer. Within days his army was decimated by pestilence; Louis himself died on 29 August, murmuring 'Jerusalem, Jerusalem'.

On 9 November Edward reached the crusaders' camp at Carthage, only to find that Louis' brother, Charles of Anjou, had come to terms with the Emir of Tunis; in return for a large indemnity he had agreed to leave the country. Baibars now had nothing more to fear from the French and could concentrate on fighting the Latins in Syria and Palestine. Thus ended St Louis' last Crusade and with it any further hope of a royal army setting out from the motherland to rescue the Franks of Outremer. Edward was disgusted by this lack of faith and purpose, and he decided to go on his own Crusade. Remembering, no doubt, his motto 'Keep troth', he exclaimed, 'By the blood of God, though all my fellow soldiers and countrymen desert me, I will enter Acre with Forvin, the groom of my palfrey, and I will keep my word and my oath to the death.' He spent the winter in Sicily, and on 9 May 1271 he landed at Acre, having travelled by ship from Palermo.

'I will keep my word and my oath to the death'

With the death of St Louis the spirituality of the age was greatly weakened. He had epitomised the medieval ideal of the Christian knight and the just king. His goodness, love of peace, and his instinctively good political judgment, disarmed all opposition; his subjects knew in their hearts that they had in St Louis an almost perfect ruler. The only criticism that could be levelled against him was the costliness of his crusading diversions. Had he been successful, Egypt would have become a French and Christian colony; it would have provided a link between Europe and Asia, and the name of St Louis would have been revered as much on the northern shores of Africa as it was in Europe. His brother, Charles of Anjou, consumed with restless ambition, was the obverse of St Louis; he was certainly not the man to carry on his brother's mission. Under St Louis, obedience to the monarchy became established in France; this obedience continued, although later kings, particularly Philip the Fair, perverted St Louis' ideals of honour and justice. Voltaire said that St Louis was the only prince who could have reformed Europe:

> He made France triumphant and well governed and in everything he did was the model for all men. His piety, which was that of an Anchorite [recluse], did not take anything away from his royal virtues; his generosity was not at the expense of a prudent administration; he knew how to combine deep political wisdom with an exact sense of justice and is perhaps the only ruler who deserves such praise. Cautious and resolute in council, fearless in battle without ever getting carried away, compassionate as if suffering had always been his lot, it is hardly ever given to a man to embody so many virtues.

It was unfortunate that he should have died just as Edward's reign was about to begin.

What St Louis failed to do with an army of 60,000 men and a fleet of 1,800 ships, could hardly be expected of Edward with his select contingent of friends and knights. He had with him about 1,000 knights, and he was later joined by his brother Edmund, John of Brittany, William of Valence and Tedaldo Visconti, Archbishop of Liège, shortly to become pope. Edward, it must be admitted, occupies a very modest place in the history of the Crusades. The importance of the sixteen months which he spent in the Holy Land lies in what he learned there and in the great fillip which the Crusade gave to his prestige and reputation. There were in fact few opportunities for him to show martial prowess, but there were plenty of occasions for him to enjoy himself. The forces at his disposal prevented him from undertaking more than a handful of raids and skirmishes, but these few have become magnified and enshrined in the annals of his deeds. He relieved Acre, where he had a tower erected, and took Nazareth, killing all the inhabitants; he led his troops across Mount Carmel to raid the

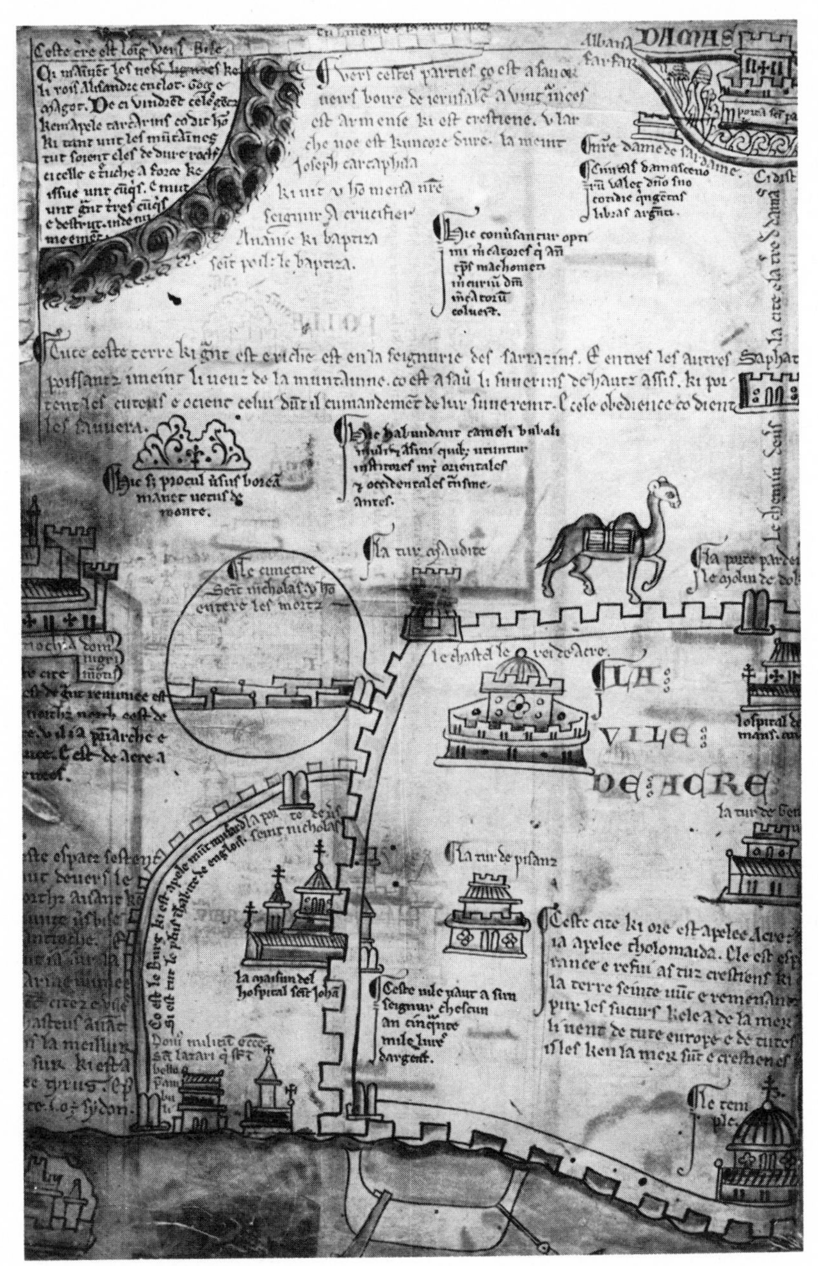

A map of Acre from a fourteenth-century manuscript. Edward relieved the city when it was on the point of surrendering to the besieging infidels.

Plain of Sharon; he tried but failed to storm the little Mameluk fortress of Qaqun which guarded the road across the hills.

The pathetic remnants of the Frankish states at this time were squeezed between the deadly Baibars in the south and the much more amenable Abaga in the north. Abaga, Mongol Khan of

Persia and Mesopotamia, was the great-grandson of Genghis Khan and a bitter enemy of Baibars and his Mameluks. He corresponded with the popes and had married a daughter of the Byzantine Emperor, Michael Palaeologus. Clement IV rightly believed that the only hope of survival for the Christian states in Syria and the Holy Land, which were now confined to Tripoli in the north, and to Beirut, Sidon, Tyre and the capital Acre in the coastal kingdom of Jerusalem, was an alliance between the Mongols, the Byzantine Emperor, Hethoum, King of Armenia, and Bohemond, Lord of Antioch and Tripoli. Edward, in pursuance of this scheme, sent an embassy to Abaga shortly after arriving in Acre. The Khan did what he could: he sent ten thousand horsemen who swept down from Anatolia into Syria. As they approached Damascus, Baibars and his superior army moved north to confront them. The Mongols were not prepared to take on the Mameluks and hastily turned back.

Edward was appalled by the petty feuding, selfishness and treachery amongst the Christians that he met in Outremer. The Venetians and Genoese, at Acre and Tyre respectively, hated each other more than the enemy; both were enjoying a flourishing trade with Baibars, providing him with slaves and weapons. The barons of Cyprus refused to follow their King Hugh to defend his mainland possession, Tripoli, against Baibars because this was held to be contrary to technicalities in feudal law. Edward soon realised that there was no realistic alternative but to compromise with the Sultan. In April 1272 a truce was concluded with Baibars to last for ten years, ten months, ten days and ten minutes. It guaranteed the Christian government of the kingdom of Jerusalem the possession of its lands on the narrow coastal plain from Acre to Sidon, together with the right to use the pilgrim road to Nazareth.

Before Edward left, he had a painful reminder of the ineffectiveness of such truces. On 16 June 1272, an Assassin, disguised as a Christian, stole into his chamber and stabbed him with a poisoned dagger. The Assassins were an order of fanatical Moslems whose chief object was to assassinate crusaders. After several days the wound grew dark and Edward was near death. The story goes that the devoted Eleanor, who had borne him a daughter in Acre, sucked the poison out of the wound. This story is now thought to lack foundation, and a more likely version of the event is that she was removed 'weeping and wailing' from the room, whilst the surgeon cut away all the darkened flesh. The resilient Edward was on horseback again within a fortnight. There was little more for him to do in the Holy Land; most of his comrades had left and he knew that his father had not much longer to live. So, on 22 September 1272, he set sail from Acre for Sicily.

Thus ended Edward's pilgrimage. He wanted to return to the Holy Land at the head of a greater Crusade, but never went back. The moral climate of Europe was changing fast, and Edward belonged as much to the new order as to the old. He was, like his father and St Louis, a loyal son of the Church and never thought for a moment of questioning papal authority, nor papal priorities such as the over-riding importance of recovering the Holy Sepulchre in Jerusalem. But the atmosphere in the West was becoming much more rational, secular and legalistic. Edward's 'crusades' in the future were to be against the Welsh, the Scots and the Jews, against those elements which interfered with the social and political unification of the nation state. The claims of his country were to come before

Crusaders approach a golden doorway, from Torsellus' *Handbook for Crusaders*. The galley is flying the crusaders' pennant and is loaded with cross-bows. On the right are two groups of mounted Saracens. Christ is depicted in a blue mandorla.

those of the international Church. He did not, it is true, purs them as ruthlessly as did his cousin Philip IV (the Fair) of Franc and when Edward was dying in Scotland, although he was n heard to murmur 'Jerusalem, Jerusalem', he did at least ask h son to send his heart with a hundred knights to be buried in t Holy Land.

Edward spent the winter of 1272 convalescing in Sicily an being entertained lavishly by its new King, Charles of Anjo While he was there he learned of the deaths of his father, h uncle Richard of Cornwall, and of his eldest son John. Whe Charles of Anjou expressed surprise that he appeared to be mo upset about the death of his father than about that of his so Edward replied that a father was irreplaceable, whereas a sc was not. Time was to show that he had spoken too confident about the availability of sons: of his four sons, three – Joh Alfonso and Henry – died young, thus clearing the way for t unfortunate reign of his youngest son, Edward.

As Edward was abroad when Henry died, he could not clai the throne for himself. Although the principle had not yet bee established, it was coming to be recognised that kingship w hereditary, that a king was a king even before he had bee anointed and crowned. The barons claimed the throne o Edward's behalf; within hours of his father's death, he w declared to have succeeded by hereditary right, and the ne reign was formally inaugurated by the Earl of Glouceste publicly swearing fealty and allegiance to King Edward. H example was followed by the barons and prelates. The regenc was vested in the Archbishop of York, Roger Mortimer, an Robert Burnell, who had been appointed by Edward as h representatives before he left England. Letters were sent out t every sheriff in the land in the King's name (although Edwar at this moment possibly jousting in Sicily, was unaware of h father's death and the baronial efforts being made on h behalf):

> The governance [*gubernaculum*] of the realm has devolved c us by hereditary succession, by the will of our magnates and by t oath of fealty they have taken to us. Henceforth we are debtor t

St Louis' coffin being carried on board ship in Tunis in preparation for its return to France. St Louis died of the plague in Tunis in August, 1270. From a fifteenth-century manuscript, *Grandes Chroniques de France*.

Pope Clement IV blessing Charles of Anjou, whom he invested with the Kingdom of Sicily in 1265. Having defeated and killed the rival Hohenstaufen claimants, Manfred and Conradino, with the help of the papacy, Charles had secured his position as King of Sicily by 1268.

> each and all to show justice and to maintain the peace. For this cause our magnates and our faithful men, in our name, have ordered our peace to be proclaimed throughout the realm.

The transfer of authority from Henry to his son could not have passed more smoothly. Edward's right to succeed to the throne was universally acknowledged; he was a national figure and had, during the previous fifteen years, given many proofs of his ability and determination to give peace to the country and prevent any fragmentation of royal authority. No baron was strong enough, as Simon de Montfort at certain moments in the late King's reign might have been, to stage a *coup d'état* or palace revolution. Nevertheless, the magnates and bishops urged Edward to hurry home. He did no such thing. So secure did he feel in the possession of his new throne that he ambled back to England, jousting all the way, only reaching London in August 1274, two years after his father's death.

The seal of Charles of Anjou, Edward's host in Sicily where he spent the winter of 1272 convalescing.

At the beginning of 1273 Edward was welcomed with great honour and magnificence by his friend, Pope Gregory x, at his Court in Orvieto. They discussed the expenses of the recent Crusade, and Edward obtained from the Pope a grant of the tenths of the clergy for three years; it was a restrospective tax to supplement the earlier financing of the Crusade and to pay outstanding creditors. They also discussed how Simon de Montfort's son, Guy, could be brought to justice. In 1271 he had, with his brother Simon, butchered Edward's cousin, Henry of Almain, the son of Richard of Cornwall, when he was hearing Mass in Viterbo. The murder was probably unpremeditated, an impulsive act by the brothers, a belated punishment for Henry's defection from the baronial cause before the Battle of Lewes. Simon was now dead, but Guy was still at large. Edward had good reason to believe that Guy was being protected by the papal authorities and he was determined

The Palace of the Popes in Orvieto, where Edward visited his old friend and ally, Tedaldo Visconti, now Pope Gregory X.

to hunt the murderer down. As a result of his pressure, the papal authorities half-heartedly pursued Guy, and in 1292 he died in a Sicilian prison.

In the spring of 1273 Edward bade farewell to the Pope and made his way northwards through Tuscany and Lombardy. The cries rang out from the crowds: 'Long live the Emperor Edward!' His fame as a Crusader turned his journey home into a triumphal progress. The legend of his pilgrimage had already begun to acquire its own independent life. He alone had had the faith and courage to carry out St Louis' design; 40,000 Frisians had followed him from Tunis (the actual number was 500). His reputation survived the failures of his expedition and his exploits were magnified. The story of how he slew his would-be assassin in Palestine with a single blow of his strong arm, and of his wife who sucked the poisoned wound, was passed from country to country; on his death songs were written about his daring exploits in the Holy Land.

OPPOSITE A page decorated with heraldry and hunting scenes from a late thirteenth-century East Anglian *Book of Hours*.

Matie

Domine labia mea a
peries et os me
um annunti
abit laudem
tuam. Deus
in adiutoriũ
meum intende. Domine ad adiuuã
me festina. Gloria patri et filio & spũi
scõ. Sicut erat in principio et nũc et
semp et in secula seculorum amen.
Deum uerum unum in trinitate et trinitatẽ
in unitate. uenite adoremus.
Venite exultemus domino iubile
mus deo salutari nr̃o preoccupem
faciem eius in confessione et in psalmis
iubilamus ei. Deum uerum unum in trini
tate et trinitatem in unitate. uenite adoremus.
Quoniam deus magnus dominus &

OPPOSITE 'The garden of love'; a romanticised picture of the joys and relaxations of courtly life from a contemporary Italian manuscript. The carefree and pleasure-filled months which Edward spent in Sicily and Italy must have been especially sweet to a man about to return to his country to take on the burdens and responsibilities of kingship.

With each step that he took towards England, Edward was leaving part of his carefree youth behind. This may have been the real reason for his slow return: he knew that the period of sowing his wild oats would soon be over. On his way to Paris he said farewell to his youth with one last, irresponsible gesture. In Burgundy he took part in a tournament organised by the Count of Châlons, an encounter which became known as the 'Little Battle of Châlons'. As a King and Crusader, Edward should not have taken part in a tournament, but the temptation was too great. He had received the Count's challenge while he was in Italy and he sent for various earls and barons from England to join him at Châlons. The Count singled him out during the encounter, and tried to drag him from his horse. The fighting became serious, but the Burgundians were finally defeated by Edward's knights, a thousand in number. After this episode, the Pope begged him to give up such dangerous sports.

After the 'Battle of Châlons', Edward went on to Paris to do homage to Philip III for the lands he held in Gascony. From Paris he went on to Gascony, where Gaston de Béarn was, as usual, in revolt, and he stayed there nearly a year. During this time he ordered the first of his great surveys into tenures, services and rights, and he made elaborate treaties for the future marriages of his children, none of which came to anything.

On 2 August 1274, Edward landed at Dover, thus setting foot in his native land after an absence of four years. He was entertained between Dover and London by Earl Gilbert of Gloucester at Tonbridge and by Earl John of Warenne at Reigate. Edward and Eleanor then went on to enter London in state. Great was the rejoicing; the town was in readiness; the city had been scrubbed and the Palace of Westminster decorated. Vast preparations had been made for the coronation feast: swans, peacocks, cranes, oxen, swine, sheep, goats, chickens and rabbits had all been prepared for the table. A chronicler records:

> To the south of the old palace, as many halls were built on all sides as room could be found for, and in them tables were set, firmly fixed in the earth, for the refreshment of magnates and

ABOVE A jousting scene from Torsellus' *Handbook for Crusaders*; one of the combatants has a raised visor and all have blunted lances and jousting saddles. Jousting was one of Edward's favourite activities, but he had little time to indulge in it once King in England.

OPPOSITE Edward I riding into London on his return from Crusade, from a fifteenth-century manuscript.

princes and nobles on the coronation day and for fifteen days afterwards; so that all men, poor and rich, coming to the ceremony, might be freely received, and nobody sent away.

On Sunday, 19 August, Edward and Eleanor walked along the carpeted paths beneath silken canopies hung with silver bells, from the palace to the Abbey Church. Here they were crowned and afterwards the splendid feast was held in Westminster Hall. In the words of one historian, 'No King since the Conquest had been welcomed with such a general sense of pleasure as Edward was on this day.'

62

A Londres vint pur sojourner
Ilorc fu tut le yver

Ilorc par maladie languist
E morut cum dieu voluist
Ilorc estoit enseuelie
A Westmouster par solempnite
Edward son fiz apres regnast
Cil tint la terre et le gardast
Cil fu de grant prowesse
Cil meintint bien ses franchises
De seint Eglise e mult l'amout
Rentes e possessions lour donout
As poures freres de religion
Sovent dona mult riche doun
Bien soet son Realme meintenir

Ed.

4 Wales 1274–94

PREVIOUS PAGES The outer walls of Beaumaris Castle on the Isle of Anglesey. Though never finished it was the most perfect and the last of the Edwardian castles.

WHEN EDWARD WAS CROWNED in Westminster Abbey at the age of thirty-five he was at the height of his powers, a proven warrior who was admired and respected at home and abroad. The Dominican friar, Nicholas Trivet, gives us a vivid description of the King at the time of his coronation in his *Annals*, written ten years after Edward's death. He was handsome and so tall that he stood head and shoulders above the rest in the common crowd. His hair, light and silvery when he was a boy, turned black in manhood. (When he grew older, it became as white as a swan.) His symmetrical features were slightly marred by a drooping eyelid, which recalled his father's appearance. In spite of a lisp, he was persuasive and ready in speech. His long arms made him a swordsman second to none, and his long shanks gave him mastery over the most spirited stallion. When he was not fighting, his passions were hawking and the chase, and he had a thorough knowledge of dogs and hawks and how to train them. He had a violent temper, but was quick to forgive. He was the hero of the troubadours in the south – they called him 'the best lance in all the world' – possessing all the virtues of the knightly class.

Wales dominated the first part of Edward's reign. The Wales of the thirteenth century was not the same country we know today whose boundaries were fixed by Henry VIII. In Edward's time everything was Wales beyond the vague and undefined limits of Cheshire, Herefordshire, Shropshire and Gloucestershire. Before the Norman conquest Wales had been ruled by a swarm of petty Celtic chieftains owing nominal allegiance to the English crown. They did not allow this lax tie to inhibit them from plundering the English border whenever an opportunity occurred. William the Conqueror and his sons changed all that. The Norman conquest of England was followed by the Norman conquest of Wales. Norman adventurers crossed over the border and drove the Welsh from the fertile plains to the barren uplands. The mutual jealousies of the petty Welsh kings made it impossible for them to resist effectively the invaders, and the Normans in their turn were soon as disunited as the Welsh they had displaced. They set up

small states which became known as the Marcher lordships, while the whole district was called the Marches of Wales. The object of these territories was to be at once a bulwark against raids from the west and a base from which to attack the Welsh. These Marcher lords were much more free than the barons of England who were kept under tight control by the Crown. In the Marches the king's writ did not run; the barons might build castles there at will without royal permission, and they were

Edward's capture of Caernarvon, the ancient centre of the kingdom of Gwynedd, was the culminating point of the war in Wales and it was here that he built Caernarvon Castle, the most magnificent of the Edwardian castles in Wales.

unencumbered by all the feudal duties to which they would have been subject had their territories been in England. One 'custom of the March' was that they could wage war at will. This they did continuously against the Welsh, with more success in the south than in the north. In the south they advanced steadily from Monmouth to Pembroke and Cardigan, along the coast and up the valleys of the Usk and Wye; in a short time they studded the region with Norman castles. The Norman kings were taking a big risk in encouraging the creation of these great feudal border baronies which might at any moment become too strong for the Crown. It was a risk they took deliberately and which they covered as best they could by choosing their kinsmen and loyal supporters for these border baronies.

The north and south of Wales was divided by a massive mountain range. The princes of Gwynedd or Snowdonia in northern Wales had as their enemy the king of England or his representative, the Earl of Chester, rather than the thrusting Marcher lords. The English kings – Henry II, King John and Henry III – were always too busy with their French possessions or with their rebellious barons at home to conquer the north by a steady process. Time and time again, when their more important preoccupations permitted it, they penetrated far west up to Snowdonia. But their armies, composed of feudal vassals of the Crown and mercenaries, were unfitted for an invasion of mountainous districts in the face of an active race of patriots. The Welsh retreated to their natural fortress of Snowdonia,

BELOW AND OPPOSITE Two hunting scenes decorate the border of the same late thirteenth-century English psalter. Edward loved hunting and hawking, and spent much time and energy laying out royal parks and trying to extend the sporting rights of the Crown.

restricted themselves to guerrilla warfare and relied on the rains and geography of the country. The royal forces were never able to establish an adequate base along the narrow coastal strip between the sea and the mountains, which were covered with dense forest. It was only Edward who, with his talent for organisation and his vast resources, was able to cut his way into northern Wales, hewing paths through the forests and maintaining his lines of communication by sea with ships brought up from Kent and Sussex.

A contemporary chronicler described the Welsh as Trojan debris swept into the wooded savagery of Cambria under the guidance of the devil. To the thirteenth-century Englishman they, like the Irish, were a nation of barbarians. Their detestable sexual promiscuity played havoc with the laws of God and the principles of hereditary succession, while their lives were spent in theft and rapine or slothful ease. In their mountain fastnesses they led a loose tribal life in their crude huts or *hafods*. Within a few hours they could pack up all their possessions and move to another valley where they would continue their treacherous and volatile way of life. In the face of such attitudes it is small wonder that, when Edward announced on 17 November 1276 his decision to go against Llewelyn, Prince of Gwynedd, as a rebel and disturber of the peace, he had the support of his English subjects.

The great chronicler, Giraldus Cambrensis or Gerald de Barri, who was of mixed Welsh and Norman blood, has described graphically the Welsh manner of fighting, their skill

Cathedral Architecture

During Edward's reign cathedral architecture was entering the Decorated style of the English Gothic period. England developed strong independent architectural styles within the Gothic tradition, which were divided into the Early English, the Decorated and the Perpendicular styles.

LEFT The octagonal Chapter House of Salisbury Cathedral, built *c.* 1265–75, was often used for the meetings of the King's Council and representative assemblies.

RIGHT Carved capitals of pillars in the Chapter House of York Cathedral, *c.* 1280.

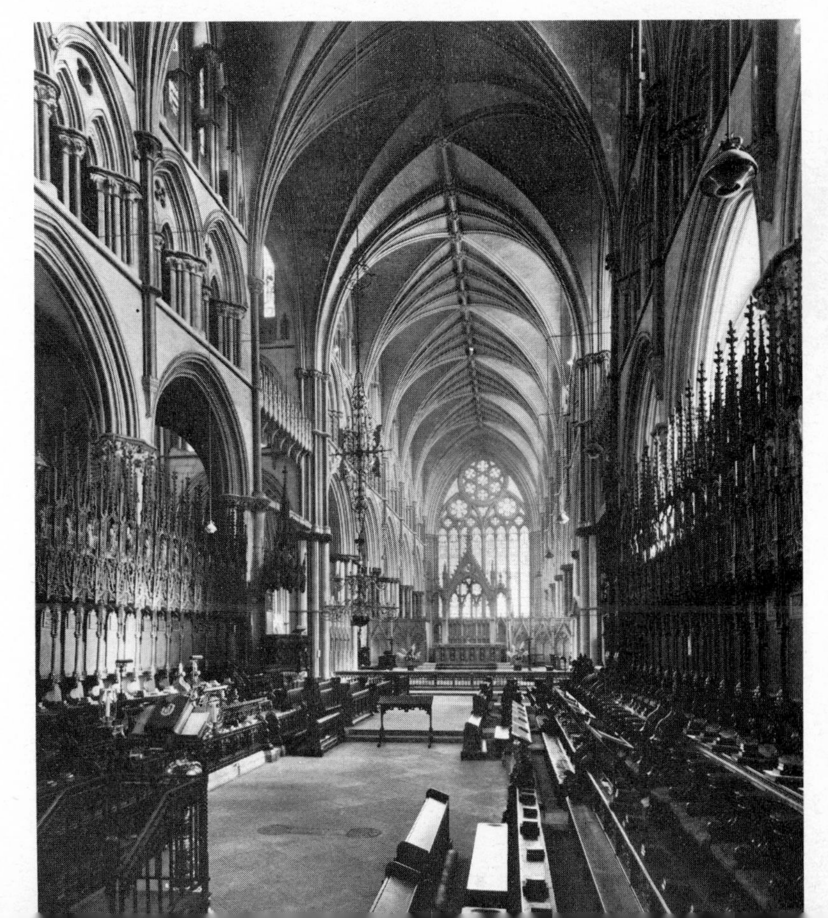

RIGHT The magnificent Angel Choir in Lincoln Cathedral, built between 1256 and 1280.

at irregular warfare, their skirmishes and surprise attacks, their light equipment of spears, bows and helmets. Above all, they loved a wild impetuous charge, generally followed by a rapid retreat to the mountains. Gerald describes the archers of Gwent, with their 'bows made of wild elm, unpolished, rude and uncouth, not only able to shoot an arrow at a great distance, but also able to inflict very severe wounds in close fight'. The men of the north fought with the traditional long spear, while those of the south fought with the long-bow. The Anglo-Normans could only meet such enemies by holding to their castles and bringing out constant reinforcements of mercenaries. The only sure way, thought Gerald, of conquering Wales was for the invaders to make use of Welsh 'friendlies'. This advice was followed by the Marcher lords: such was the disunity amongst the southern Welsh that they were perfectly happy to fight under the banners of their lords and help them to subjugate their fellow countrymen. The men of Gwent, who had fought fiercely before being subdued by William de Braose, the powerful Marcher lord, became later the most valuable of Edward's allies: it was from them that the English learned how to use the long-bow, which became their chief weapon.

The Braose family, who came from Normandy, had their headquarters at Abergavenny; through marriage they acquired Brecknock and upper Gwent; they conquered as far as Builth (where one of the castles was to be completely rebuilt by Edward), thus reaching the territory of the Mortimers in the Middle March. The Marcher lands changed hands from time to time during the twelfth and thirteenth centuries, generally through marriage rather than conquest. Gilbert Fitzgerald de Clare was given Cardigan and Pembroke by Henry I; later his family lost Cardigan but gained Glamorgan and Gloucester. Clare, Hastings, Valence, Bigod, Bohun, Mortimer, Lacy, Fitzalan, Warenne – these are the famous families that at different times held what was, until recently, Shropshire, Denbigh, Monmouth, Glamorgan, Carmarthen, Cardigan and Pembroke. The Marcher lords and the south Welsh princes co-existed uneasily, but together they encircled the impregnable principality of Gwynedd or Snowdonia. If the country were ever to be united by a Welsh prince, he would have to be a strong lord of Gwynedd, the 'prince of Aberffraw and North Wales', as he was officially styled.

Llewelyn ap Iorwerth, the Great, was such a strong prince. He seized his opportunity when England was weakened and divided by the struggle between King John and his rebellious barons, and when the Lord Rhys, Prince of Deheubarth in south Wales, died. The Lord Rhys had had a friendly attitude to the English and had worked for the gradual assimilation of Welsh and Marcher lordships under the overlordship of the English Crown. Llewelyn the Great reversed this policy. Although his wife was a daughter of King John and his own daughters had married Marcher lords, he was at heart a Welsh patriot and he wanted the English out of Wales. He devastated the Marches in

The wild and rocky fastnesses of Gwynedd where the Welsh were able to evade their English persecutors.

the south and east, destroying castles as he went. At one moment in the struggle with John and the Marcher barons he was master of most of the country.

Llewelyn the Great died in 1240, having created a tradition of Welsh unity which his grandson, Llewelyn ap Gruffydd, took up later. In the meantime the Marcher lords fought back, regaining their lands and rebuilding their castles. Henry compelled the young Llewelyn to sign in 1247, the year after he became Prince of Gwynedd, the Treaty of Woodstock; in it he agreed that he held north Wales in fee to the King of England, and he surrendered all the coastal lands between Chester and the Conway Valley known as the Four Cantreds. His principality was now much smaller than the one which his grandfather had inherited.

The question of lordship was one which confused and bedevilled relations between the English king, the Welsh princes and the barons of the Marches. Did Llewelyn and the other Welsh princes hold their principalities in fee of the English Crown? If they did, they were vassals of the English king, like the great earls of the realm, and it was their duty to pay him homage. Llewelyn ap Gruffydd's view was that he held his principality under Edward's royal power, but that its rights were, in his own words, 'entirely separate from the rights' of England. He did not, for example, have to obtain royal approval, as did the English feudal barons, for sheltering fugitives, building castles and creating markets. Any dispute between him and his overlord should be settled on the border by arbitrators appointed by each side and he was at liberty to deal with his vassals according to Welsh law. Edward thought differently: although he recognised the special nature of Welsh law and customs, he insisted on his right to hear Welsh petitions at Westminster and to adjudicate upon them 'according to God and Justice and depending upon what the prelates and magnates of this realm advise, especially as no one supposes that such prudent men will give the King advice dissonant with or contrary to reason'.

Llewelyn's grandfather, Llewelyn the Great, had not

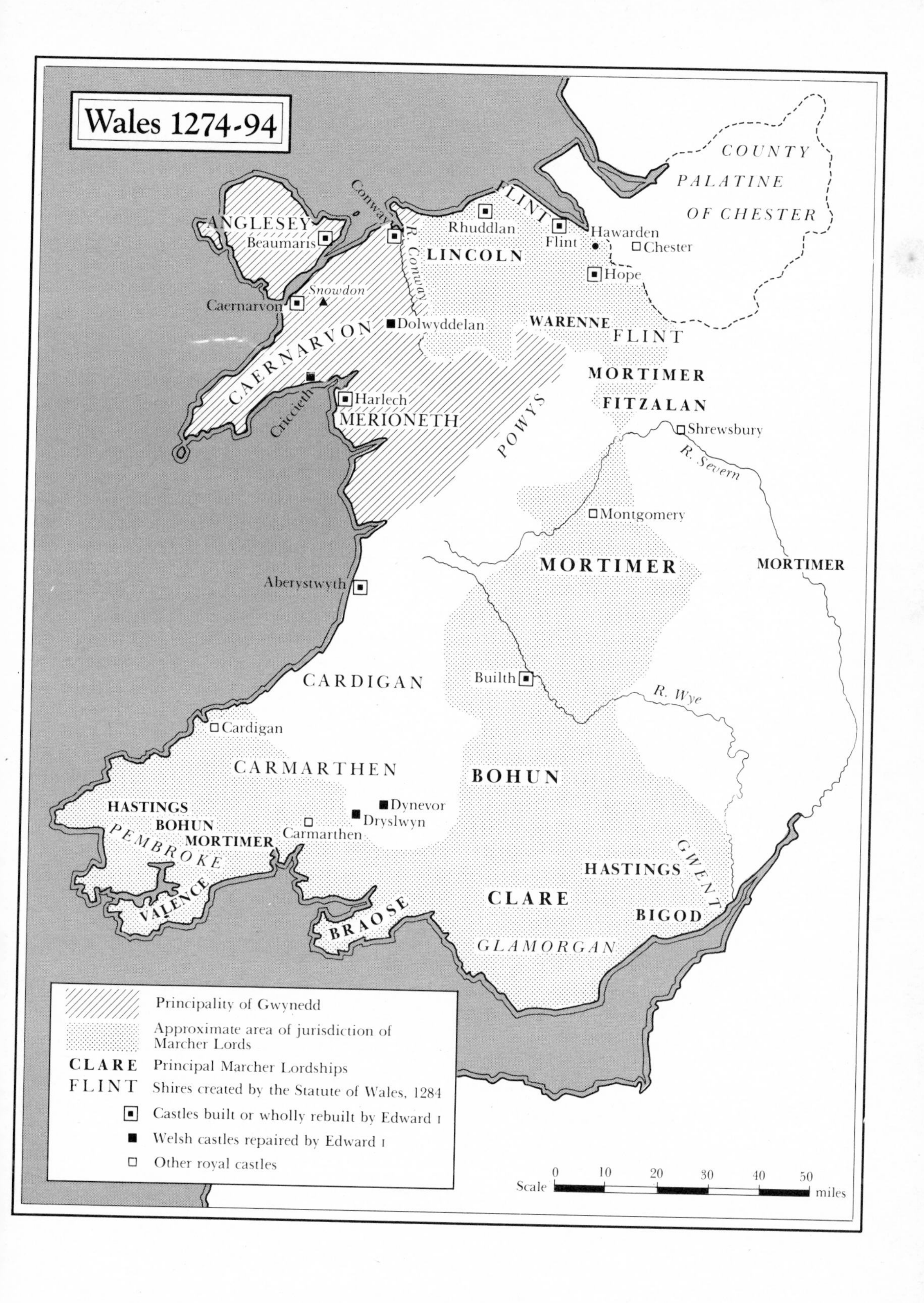
Wales 1274-94
ANGLESEY
Beaumaris
Conway
R. Conway
Rhuddlan
FLINT
Flint
Hawarden
Chester
COUNTY
PALATINE
OF CHESTER
LINCOLN
Hope
Snowdon
Caernarvon
Dolwyddelan
WARENNE
FLINT
CAERNARVON
MORTIMER
FITZALAN
Criccieth
Harlech
MERIONETH
POWYS
Shrewsbury
R. Severn
Montgomery
MORTIMER
MORTIMER
Aberystwyth
CARDIGAN
Builth
R. Wye
Cardigan
CARMARTHEN
BOHUN
HASTINGS
BOHUN
MORTIMER
PEMBROKE
Dynevor
Dryslwyn
Carmarthen
GWENT
HASTINGS
CLARE
BIGOD
VALENCE
BRAOSE
GLAMORGAN
Principality of Gwynedd
Approximate area of jurisdiction of Marcher Lords
CLARE Principal Marcher Lordships
FLINT Shires created by the Statute of Wales, 1284
Castles built or wholly rebuilt by Edward I
Welsh castles repaired by Edward I
Other royal castles
Scale
0
10
20
30
40
50
miles

Two sketches by Matthew Paris of scenes in Welsh history.

OPPOSITE Llewelyn the Great on his deathbed in 1240, with his grandsons, Llewelyn ap Gruffydd and David, in attendance.

RIGHT Llewelyn ap Gruffydd falls when trying to escape from the Tower of London where he was imprisoned by Henry III in 1244.

hesitated, when it served his own interests, to turn to Henry III and seek his judgment as overlord, as when, for instance, he wished to be succeeded by David, his son by King John's daughter Joan, rather than by his troublesome, illegitimate elder son Gruffydd. In Welsh law Gruffydd's illegitimacy was not a disability to the succession, but feudal practice and English law did not permit it. Llewelyn, therefore, appealed to Henry III, and by so doing he admitted the superior validity of English law and his dependence upon the Crown. On the other hand, he required the Welsh magnates to do homage to David as his heir, although David had not done homage to Henry and the magnates owed homage to the King as his tenants-in-chief. Sometimes royal writ and sometimes Welsh custom prevailed. This lack of clarity as to which law governed Anglo-Welsh matters provided the perfect excuse for aggression on both sides.

In 1254 Henry III gave the fifteen-year-old Edward the

county palatine of Chester and all the Crown lands in Wales, including the Four Cantreds of Perfeddwled gained in the treaty of 1247. At the same time he was granted Ireland, the Channel Islands and Gascony, as well as certain English cities such as Bristol, Stamford and Grantham. In those days provision for a king's son was not made by grants from a civil list, but by settling upon him large estates and territories which, if well administered, would provide him with an adequate income. Another purpose of these grants was to give the young lord some practical experience of government in out-lying, semi-independent territories which were not, strictly speaking, part of the main kingdom. Edward's appanage, although enormous, was unprofitable and nearly ungovernable. Ireland was in a state of hopeless confusion and it was beyond the ability of Edward and his advisers to grapple with the difficulties in that country. They preferred instead to concentrate their efforts on the smaller and more accessible territory of Wales.

It was to be Edward's policy as king to try to bring the whole of the British islands under the rule of the Crown. That he displayed such single-mindedness towards this end may be attributed to his early experiences in Wales. The starting-point for the reduction of his Welsh lands was the earldom of Chester. Chester was a palatine earldom, set up by William the Conqueror to keep the wild Welsh in check. The word 'palatine' came to England from Germany and was applied to certain counties where the earls or rulers enjoyed exceptional powers; they acted as independent princes, although they owed homage and fealty to the king. The most important of the counties palatine were Chester and Durham. The great line of earls of Chester became extinct with the death of John the Scot in 1237 and the earldom 'escheated' to the Crown. Henry was therefore able, by exercising the royal prerogative of the bestowal of lapsed fiefs, to invest Edward with the rich and powerful palatinate. As Earl of Chester he was in a position to make good the grant of 'Wales'.

In fact, Edward's efforts to establish himself in Wales at this time were an abysmal failure: the Welsh revolted against the

Portrait of Edward I from a French chronicle of the world dating from the fifteenth century.

rapacity and violence of his officials and tax collectors and appealed to Llewelyn ap Gruffydd to rescue them. Llewelyn used their plea as the occasion for attempting to regain those lands which had been lost since his grandfather's death. He assumed the title 'Prince of Wales' in 1258 and during the next few years he exploited the troubled situation in England to establish his authority throughout Wales. It is interesting that the uprising was directed against Edward himself rather than against the English as a whole. He showed himself incapable of dealing with the Welsh rebels; the Marcher lords who supported the baronial cause looked on with indifference, although this turned to alarm when Llewelyn entered into an alliance with Simon de Montfort. This act proved to be Simon's undoing; the Marcher lords, hitherto solid for reform, moved to the royalist side. When the baronial war was over, the Peace of Montgomery in 1267 confirmed Llewelyn's title as Prince of Wales, admitted his overlordship of the other Welsh princes and recognised all his conquests. No Welsh prince had ever enjoyed such power and prestige as Llewelyn did when Henry died in 1272.

It is essential to bear in mind the division of Wales into the principality (established by the Peace of Montgomery) and the Marches if we wish to understand Edward's Welsh policy. In his day the principality meant only those districts ruled by the Prince of Wales, Llewelyn ap Gruffydd, consisting of the modern shires of Anglesey, Caernarvon and Merioneth. The English Crown lands were the Four Cantreds (Denbighshire and Flintshire) and large parts of Cardiganshire and Carmarthenshire. The most important of the Welsh Marcher lordships were the palatine earldom of Pembroke and the lordships of Glamorgan, whose lords were the Earls of Gloucester. Next in importance was the lordship of Brecon, an appendage to the earldom of Hereford. Further north the Mortimers controlled Shropshire and the Middle Marches. Thus all southern and eastern Wales was March land.

Edward did not return from the Holy Land with the intention of conquering Wales. Was his later policy towards that country that of an imaginative and constructive conqueror or of a ruthless and bloodthirsty tyrant? We know enough about Edward to be able to see some truth in both viewpoints. His relations with Llewelyn are rather perplexing: sometimes they were friends, sometimes enemies. King and Prince had different ideas about the nature of Llewelyn's status as a dependent of the English Crown. For Edward this did not differ much from that of other great lords, who were bound to do homage for their lands and to obtain royal permission for certain actions. Llewelyn put his case to Edward in these words: 'You know well that the rights of our principality are entirely separate from the rights of your kingdom, although we hold our principality under your royal power.' This was in a letter protesting that Edward's lieutenants had forbidden him to build a castle on his own lands.

Llewelyn did not go to Edward's coronation at Westminster and he refused repeatedly to do homage on the grounds that

Edward was sheltering his enemies. One such was his own brother David and the other was Gruffydd ap Gwenwynwyn, Lord of Powys, both of whom had been plotting to overthrow Llewelyn. Another incident exacerbated feeling on both sides. Ten years earlier, in the intoxicating days of his alliance with Simon de Montfort, Llewelyn had been engaged to Simon's daughter Eleanor. Now he was arranging for her to come to Wales for the marriage. Edward had the ship she was travelling in captured and Eleanor was taken to Windsor, with the intention that she should be kept hostage until Llewelyn should submit and do homage. Llewelyn appeared to be reliving the days of the barons' war with the hope of finally throwing off English overlordship. Edward's patience was at an end and, on 12 November 1276, he pronounced Llewelyn contumacious and decided to 'go against him as a rebel and a disturber of the peace'. Llewelyn was quickly defeated, did homage and accepted peace terms which reduced the principality to the western part of Snowdonia. He then married Eleanor de Montfort at Worcester with much ceremony and at the King's expense.

'Go against him as a rebel and a disturber of the peace'

It looked as if peace had come at long last. But both sides had reckoned without Llewelyn's restless brother David, the cause of the outbreak of war in 1282. Apparently dissatisfied with the amount of territory which Edward had bestowed upon him, he swept down one night upon Hawarden; within a few days all north Wales had risen.

Edward acted quickly to suppress Wales' last serious attempt at independence. He was supported wholeheartedly by his barons, the Church and the people of England. Llewelyn, who soon joined his brother in rebellion, underestimated the profound wish of the English for an end to civil strife. He also underestimated the military skill and determination of Edward who applied naval tactics to the problem of the conquest of Wales. He poured into the Welsh campaign the vast resources of his realm. Llewelyn was blockaded in his rocky mountain stronghold of Snowdonia; he slipped through the blockading forces to organise a counter-movement in the Wye Valley.

Soldiers attacking a castle; two of the besiegers are mining the castle walls.

Here, in December 1282, not far from Builth, he was killed in a chance encounter with a border force. With his death the cause of Welsh independence collapsed.

Let the *Chronicle of Lanercost* tell us how Edward dealt with Llewelyn and his brother David, captured soon afterwards. Lanercost was an Augustinian priory in Cumberland not far from the Scottish border. The *Chronicle*, pious and royalist in tone, consists of the jottings of Augustinian canons who recorded history as they heard it. In relation to Welsh events, it expresses the contempt and boredom with which the English greeted yet another uprising in that lawless land, and their relief that Edward had finally disposed of the unreliable and volatile Llewelyn.

> In the unlucky course of that year [1283] the Welsh nation broke over their borders carrying fire and sword among the people ... their prince Llewelyn, deceived by the advice of his brother David, fiercely attacked his lord the king ... David persuaded his brother to rebel, trusting after the act to conciliate the King by his [David's] proved devotion. Having therefore raised an army, the King went in person to Wales, accompanied by gallant men ... at this time the head of Llewelyn was sent to the King, although he would not have approved of this being done. However, it was taken to the Tower of London and fixed upon a stake. Arising from these events, the King took proceedings against the traitor David. He resumed the campaign and, determined to exterminate the whole people of the nation, he caused them to be beset by land and sea in the district of Snowdon with a great fleet, so that by famine he might crush those strong hearts which relied upon safety in stones and rocks.

David was hunted down and captured in the Welsh hills. Edward refused to see him and asked the barons who had assembled in Shrewsbury to decide his fate. He had the distinction of being the first political prisoner to be hanged, drawn and quartered. The *Chronicle* describes the scene with some relish:

> David was first drawn as a traitor, then hanged as a thief; thirdly, he was beheaded alive, and his entrails burnt as an incendiary and homicide; fourthly, his limbs were cut into four parts as the penalty of a rebel, and exposed in four of the ceremonial places in England as a spectacle; to wit – the right arm with a ring on the finger in York; the left arm in Bristol; the right leg and hip at Northampton; the left leg at Hereford. But the villain's head was bound with iron, lest it should fall to pieces from putrefaction, and set conspicuously upon a long spear-shaft for the mockery of London.

By the Statute of Wales in 1284 the independent principality came to an end; the shire system was introduced in those parts where it did not already exist; and the country was brought under the English legal system. On 25 April 1284, Eleanor of Castile gave birth to a Welsh-born son, Edward of Caernarvon, the future King. In 1301 the young Edward was proclaimed the first English Prince of Wales; he was about the same age as his father had been when Henry endowed him with all the royal lands of Wales.

Edward's Welsh campaign of 1282–3 was of incalculable importance in determining the main features of his reign. It also brought out clearly certain contradictory aspects of the King's complex character. History's picture of Edward is that of a great warrior, lawgiver and administrator. He was fated to wage war for most of his life; as a young man he took a reckless delight in combat, whether against the barons at Lewes and Evesham, the Moslems in Outremer, or the Burgundians at the 'Little Battle of Châlons'. His later wars against the Welsh, the French and the Scots were of a different nature: they were an unavoidable consequence of his determination to impose his royal authority in every corner of his kingdom, including his duchy of Gascony. It is true that the baronial wars were also about royal authority, but on that occasion Edward was fundamentally in agreement with the cause of the baronial reformers and he fought them out of filial loyalty and an understandable desire to preserve his own inheritance.

Throughout Edward's reign England was on a permanent war footing. He needed large armies, it being his policy to crush his enemies by sheer weight of numbers. Money and men were needed to finance and wage these wars, but how and where were they to be found? The campaigns were long and the feudal practice of providing the king with knights for a week or two of each year was inadequate. The Italian merchant bankers, Riccardi of Lucca and the Frescobaldi of Florence, might help finance the odd Crusade and campaign, but not these wars to the death with stubborn races who refused to perceive the benefits of English rule. The country had to be organised on a massive scale to find the necessary armies, materials and money.

With Edward's Welsh wars the age of the foot-archers was dawning: Lewes and Evesham were the last two battles in

Edward of Caernarvon created Prince of Wales by his father in 1301. This event, which was welcomed by many of the Welsh, was a symbol of a new and more peaceful period in the relations between England and Wales.

'Castles should be built as centres of permanent occupation'

England where the mailed horseman was supreme. Edward recognised the superiority of the south Welsh archers, and without them he would never have subdued their country. Giraldus Cambrensis had said that there was only one policy which would lead to the successful conquest of Wales: 'Castles should be built as centres of permanent occupation, and in the field, lances and bows should be combined.' Edward followed his advice on both these points: the combination of the heavy Anglo-Norman horse with its mailed rider and skilled Welsh archers was irresistible. Edward perfected these tactics – archers interlaced with horse – in Wales, Scotland and finally in France. He and his Welsh archers laid the foundations of the English triumphs in the Hundred Years' War. However, the size of his armies was not exceeded until the seventeenth century. In Wales he had at times 15,000 foot in royal pay, of whom 9,000 were Welsh; at one period he had over 30,000 infantry in various parts of Wales. This sounds all the more impressive when it is realised that the largest force raised in Queen Elizabeth's reign was one of 12,000 destined for Ireland.

The other piece of advice that Edward took from Giraldus Cambrensis was the construction of a splendid chain of castles in north Wales. He built eight castles altogether, all of which were begun and completed between 1277 and 1295. They may still be seen today, remarkably complete, at Caernarvon, Conway and Beaumaris, and only a little less so at Rhuddlan and Harlech. Of the other Edwardian castles, Flint, Aberystwyth and Hope have suffered more severely. Of the castle of Builth, only the Norman earthworks now remain, rising beside the River Wye. Five of these castles – Aberystwyth, Flint, Rhuddlan, Conway and Caernarvon – were more than just castles: they were castles integrated with fortified towns or *bastides* and were closely connected in structure with Edward's new towns in Gascony which are described in Chapter 6. Of these, the most splendid and elaborate were Conway and Caernarvon.

The castles in Wales, together with the Eleanor Crosses, constitute Edward's architectural legacy in Britain. Little or nothing remains of his other building enterprises: Vale Royal, the huge Cistercian abbey in Cheshire which he founded in fulfilment of a vow made on a rough sea journey, has disappeared without trace; his alterations and additions to the Tower of London and Westminster Abbey have been restored beyond recognition. The Welsh castles on the other hand, stripped as they are of their plaster, timber and glass, of their lead roofs and their iron grilles, have come down to us almost structurally unaltered from the time of their building. They show that Edward had, like his father, his own style of magnificence. His castles were not simply sober functional fortresses, placed there for the sole purpose of over-awing the natives: they were great imaginative and romantic structures, as well as symbols of his political and military triumphs.

As his predecessors had encouraged the cult of Edward the Confessor to emphasise their links with the Anglo-Saxon monarchy, so Edward romanticised his wars in Wales by invoking the Arthurian legend. It may have been his conscious policy to set himself up as a new Arthur: he carried on his Crusade a book about the Grail romances; he held a great tournament or round table at Nefyn in Caernarvonshire after the birth of Edward of Caernarvon; he accepted the crown of King Arthur, a Welsh national treasure; and he opened the supposed tombs of Arthur and Guinevere at Glastonbury and had their bodies reburied. He had not forgotten that the Provençal poets had called him 'the best lance in all the world', and he encouraged, knowing the value of propaganda, the popular mythologising of his jousts, feasts and military exploits. His castles would add to the grandeur and mystery of a legendary past.

'The best lance in all the world'

Edward's castle-building was unusual in being a medieval state enterprise involving, like his Welsh campaign, more men, money and time than had ever been expended before. It appears almost incongruous that these mighty fortresses, with their beautiful and exotic decorations, should have been erected with the main purpose of keeping surveillance on those elusive Welshmen, scurrying up and down their mountain valleys like

OVERLEAF Caerphilly Castle in mid-Glamorgan built between 1268 and 1277 by Gilbert de Clare, richest of the Marcher Lords. It was the earliest concentric castle in Britain, a precursor to those built by Edward and one on which he based many of his designs.

nomadic pixies. In their ungratitude they were to attempt to wreck several of them in an uprising in 1294.

How many men worked on these castles, how much did they cost and how were they financed? The answers to these questions are to be found in the Pipe Rolls, into which the particulars of the buildings were entered. Roughly £80,000 was spent on all eight castles up to the time of the appointment of Edward of Caernarvon as Prince of Wales. They varied in their size and scale of elaboration from the modest simplicity of Builth to the towering magnificence of Conway. The cost of Caernarvon was in the region of £20,000. Edward spent more than £80,000 on the vanished abbey of Vale Royal. The money for the castles came from the King's wardrobe and from Ireland – the Welsh themselves contributed practically nothing. The labour force – masons, quarriers, carpenters, diggers, smiths, carters and the rest – was drawn from all over England and worked for a seven-month season. There were always around 2,500 to 3,500 men at work during the season, sometimes all together on a single site, sometimes working on several castles at the same time. It was certainly a large work force when one considers that it was taken from a population hardly more than a tenth of its present level.

Edward's right-hand man during this castle-building period was Master James of St George. He had huge responsibilities, both administrative and technical. He was not only an architect, but ran from Harlech Castle, which he had built and of which he was Constable, the complex programme for the building and financing of all the Welsh castles. He was neither English (nor Welsh!) but a Savoyard from that vanished state which few of us can accurately situate on the map. He was not, however, one of the detested Savoyard relatives of Eleanor of Provence, those objects of Henry's munificence. Edward, like his father, gave jobs to foreigners, but they were professionals and technicians rather than aristocrats. He did not discriminate against his royal Continental kinsmen, but only used them if they had some kind of ability.

OPPOSITE Harlech Castle was placed on a superb natural site. In the rebellion of 1294, thirty-seven men defended Harlech against the entire Welsh army.

Those with a knowledge of medieval architecture will recognise that the Edwardian castles are not the work of a master mason with an English background: there is nothing English about the distinctive windows of Harlech, the pinnacles and crenellations of Conway, the shape of the arches of Beaumaris, Caernarvon and Flint. They have their exact parallels or counterparts in Savoy, where James of St George practised and where he probably first met Edward. This would have been in June 1273 after Edward had left Gregory X at Orvieto and was on his way to take part in the tournament at Châlons. Between these two episodes he crossed the Alps and entered the principality of his great-uncle, Philip of Savoy. Savoy in those days covered territories which are now partly in western Switzerland, partly in north-west Italy and partly in eastern France. The brothers of Philip were those unpopular Savoyards, Peter of Savoy, and Boniface, Archbishop of Canterbury. His nephew, Amadeus of Savoy, was later to fight for Edward in his Welsh wars of 1277 and 1282. When Edward called on Philip in the summer of 1273 at his agreeable castle in the Isère, St Georges-d'Espéranches, the elderly count did homage to his great-nephew for the overlordship of Avigliana and Susa near Turin, and one or two other Alpine towns and castles. They were fiefs that had, for some reason or other, been granted to Henry thirty years earlier. It was there that Edward probably first noticed the skill of Philip's master of works, James of St George, who was responsible for the basic design of all the great Edwardian castles in Wales, including Caernarvon. In the winter of 1287 he joined the King in Gascony and stayed there until the Court returned to England in 1289. In 1298 the outbreak of war with Scotland gave him further architectural opportunities. For over twenty years, then, he was Edward's leading master mason and military engineer. He applied the style and techniques of his native Savoy to castles and *bastides* in Wales, Gascony, England and Scotland.

The architectural parallels between the military works and town walls in Savoy and those of the same period in Wales are striking. The castles of Chillon (home of Byron's prisoner) on

Conway Castle has an ideal position, being built on a huge slab of rock above a sheltered tidal harbour.

Lake Geneva, Saillon in the Valais, Grandson on Lake Neuchâtel, St Georges-d'Espéranches in Isère, La Bâtiaz in the Valais, San Giorgio in Val di Susa, Yverdon and Champvent anticipate the main features of Edward's castles – the laying of the stones, the arches and embrasures, the types of garderobe construction, the filials on the battlements, the basic quadrangular plans. Castle connoisseurs can spot affinities between Harlech and Chillon, Conway and St Georges-d'Espéranches, Beaumaris and Saillon, Yverdon and Flint, although they are more than a thousand miles distant from one another.

Caernarvon, the most fabulous castle of all, was to be the memorial and symbol of past greatness and the viceregal centre of a new order. Fabulous it indeed was, for it reached back not to a recent but to a legendary past. The Welsh associated the ruins of Roman Segontium, the old Caernarvon, with an age-old antiquity which linked the castle of Arfon with imperial

Rome. In 1283 a body thought to be that of Magnus Maximus, father of the Emperor Constantine, was found at Caernarvon and Edward ordered it to be buried in the church. Edward had certainly read the Mabinogian tales, one of which told of Maximus' dream which took him from Rome to a land of high mountains: he saw a river flowing into the sea and facing the land was an island; at the mouth of the river was a great fortified city and in the city a great fort, the fairest man ever saw, and great towers of many colours on the fort; and in its hall a chair of ivory with two golden eagles. Edward now proceeded, with the help of Master James of St George, to build 'the fairest fort man ever saw' at the mouth of the River Seiont and opposite the island of Anglesey. Edward, like Ludwig of Bavaria, turned his dreams into stone; his dreams, however, were not escapist flights of morbid fancy, but the imaginative blending of political reality with national legend.

The outward apearance of Caernarvon is dramatically

Building a castle; detail of carvings in the Chapter House of Salisbury Cathedral.

different from that of its great contemporaries. The difference lies chiefly in its polygonal instead of rounded towers and in the prominent patterning of its walls with bands of differently coloured stone. Both these features were unique in England. Banded masonry was often to be found in Italian medieval architecture, but for its use in conjunction with polygonal towers there was one famous precedent: the tile-laced Theodosian walls of Constantinople, the Emperor Constantine's own city. It is clear that it was Edward's intention from the outset to build a palace-castle which would recall Caernarvon's legendary past by reflecting in its symbolism its Roman origins. So Edward, that formidable ruler of unbending will and untiring persistence, was a romantic too; we should remember this when we read of his more prosaic achievements as an administrator and lawgiver.

Edwar
dus.1.

5
The English Justinian 1274-1307

PREVIOUS PAGES A woodcut of Edward I showing him as he was remembered by posterity: a strong warrior-king and determined law-maker.

THE THIRTEENTH CENTURY was the age of the lawyer and the legislator. One of the most important results of the intellectual renaissance of the twelfth century was a revived interest in Roman law. Throughout Europe universities were springing up with active legal faculties. At the University of Bologna a comprehensive survey of Roman law was begun, and before long two great systems had emerged: civil (Roman) law and canon law – the law of the emperors and the law of the popes. Roman law was practised in the Italian city states, but its influence outside Italy was academic until the thirteenth century. English lawyers, Henry de Bracton for example, knew Roman law well, but the most important effect of its influence in England was the codification of English law, rather than the introduction of the principles of Roman law. At the end of Edward's reign there was a flight from codification and a return to practice and judge-made law. This became so natural a part of the country's legal structure that, when the fifteenth century saw the 'reception' of Roman law all over the Continent, England remained unaffected.

In England lawyers became increasingly conscious of the imperfections of their chaotic feudal laws and customs, so they tried to mould them into an harmonious structure which would hold its own with the majestic edifices of civil and canon law. The first systematic exposition of English law was written by Henry de Bracton in the reign of Henry III. Edward carried on this great work by initiating much new legislation, and the years 1274 to 1290 are known as the years of the statutes. Their significance has been differently interpreted by historians. His legislation was in the main concerned with the establishment of the rights of the Crown and the provision of remedies against the usurpation of these rights by the barons. The statutes attempted to define exactly the boundary between rights and feudal privileges (as in *Quo Warranto*) and also to define feudal tenures, whenever possible to the King's advantage (as in the Statute of Mortmain, *De Donis Conditionalibus* and *Quia Emptores*). Edward's legislation has sometimes been described as conservative but revolutionary, meaning that its general effect was to eliminate feudalism from English life. Like other monarchs of the late thirteenth century, Edward disliked any authority which did not emanate from himself (hence his conflicts with the Church) and this attitude could, in some eyes, mean that he was consciously attempting to replace the feudal by a monarchical structure of society. This, of course, cannot be true: although towards the end of the thirteenth century feudalism was beginning to disappear, Edward would have been the last person to perceive it. He accepted the assumptions of his time, one of which was that people lived in a feudal society.

The essential element of feudalism was the feudal bond between the lord and his vassal. The term comes from the Latin word *feodum* or *feudum*, meaning a fee or fief. The fief was generally a plot of land, although it could be a revenue in money or kind. In return for the fief, the man became the vassal of his lord. As an act of homage he knelt before his lord and placed his hands in those of his lord. Then he rose to his feet and swore a solemn oath of fealty which bound him to keep faith and be true to his lord. He then received from his lord ceremonial investiture with the fief.

Although the fief had not originally been hereditary, it became before long an inherent part of the feudal contract that the grant was hereditable. As long as the vassal and his heirs performed those duties which they had assumed by doing homage, their right and title to the fief was secure. The most characteristic duty was that of military service, which meant appearing on the field when summoned with a certain number of men, and remaining a specified length of time. England was covered with a network of these fiefs rising from the knight's fee at the bottom of the social scale, to the king at the top. The king was the supreme landowner, holding his kingdom from God. The feudal state was one where private law had usurped the place of public law. Services were private and local between the lord and his vassal. Although the king was the supreme lord, the practical expression of his authority was limited by the self-contained feudal structure.

The supreme landowner, holding his kingdom from God

Edward tried, by the steady, ruthless use of the royal prerogative to enhance his own power at the expense of traditional feudal conventions. This, as much as a desire for social justice, was the motive for the great statutes of his reign. He was greedy for power and the constant object of his legislation was the exaltation of the royal prerogative. He took however a broader and more comprehensive view of authority than had his father or grandfather. He wished to rule the State, but at the same time he wanted to take his subjects into partnership with him, provided that they recognised his royal rights. In this spirit he accepted the rights and privileges of different classes, while being very careful not to permit any extension of feudal authority. He fought hard any movement which, in his view, threatened the inalienable supremacy of the Crown. He was prepared to co-operate with the barons in enforcing their feudal rights but would never admit that the feudal tenure of land permitted the vassal to set up a little state within the State. Edward narrowly circumscribed every old right and refused to recognise any new ones.

As we have seen, discontent with royal government had prompted demands for a larger voice in advising the King. In 1258 it amounted to a claim to share his executive power. The Oxford Parliament set up a baronial oligarchy which was almost as oppressive as royal power; but the bold experiment of the Provisions of Oxford failed and the King's right to appoint his own advisers was successfully reaffirmed. Long before that, however – indeed since the reign of King John – the idea of a limited monarchy controlled by a national council and reigning in accordance with the principles of Magna Charta, had been gradually finding a place in the minds of Englishmen. The clash of interests between the king and the barons made it necessary for both to widen their support and to take into partnership the lesser landholders and the merchants and traders of the towns. Edward carried on Simon de Montfort's policy of trusting the people at large: he retained Simon's innovation of enlarging the circle of those who were summoned to give advice to the King or, during his fifteen months of power, to the baronial council.

OPPOSITE Westminster Hall: frequently the seat of Parliament in the Middle Ages and the chief law court of England until the Strand law courts were completed in 1870.

Their motives in doing this were rather different: Simon enlarged the advisory circle to win support for his cause, while Edward was trying to find fresh sources of taxation.

The word Parliament came to be used for those occasions when the king took counsel with a larger number of advisers than usual; they held 'parleys' or talks. Edward's early Parliaments were chaotic and haphazard affairs: one year he would assemble the knights of the shires, the next just the barons and bishops. The composition of a Parliament seemed to depend upon the nature of the business to be laid before it. However, towards the end of his reign the national council or Parliament was not considered complete unless it contained representatives of the three estates.

The main reason why Parliament became more 'popular' in composition during the years of emergency was that Edward felt that he could only meet his difficulties if he had the support of the nation as a whole. It was only by national grants of money that he could get the better of his enemies in France and Scotland. He enunciated the maxim that what touches all should be approved by all. The most comprehensive assembly ever to have been summoned in England was in 1295, when money was needed for the war against Philip the Fair. The earls and barons came as a matter of course; by their side gathered two knights chosen by the popular court of each shire and two citizens or burgesses from every city or borough town. The clergy also attended in full force: archbishops, bishops, abbots, deans, archdeacons and representatives of the parochial clergy of each diocese. The result was a Parliament genuinely representing the three estates – the barons for the lords temporal, the clergy for the lords spiritual, and the knights and burgesses for the wider community of the well-to-do. This Parliament came to be looked on as a model for succeeding ages.

During part of Edward's reign (1274–86), he summoned Parliaments about twice a year; these came to be known as the Easter Parliament and the Michaelmas Parliament. The battle for royal authority having previously been won, there was as yet no question of the monarchy being limited by Parliament any more than by the barons in council. We should also remember that they were summoned not in deference to any principle, but generally to raise money. Edward, although personally economical, was throughout his reign deeply in debt. His pecuniary exigencies left their unfortunate influence on his popularity while he lived, and on the reputation which he left behind him. He was to do many harsh, short-sighted, devious things to get himself out of tight financial corners, and his tendency to resort to legal captiousness always showed itself on these occasions. This weakness was brought into prominence by the character of his advisers: this was the age of the lawyer and Edward's advisers tended to be lawyers rather than churchmen. The great distinguishing mark of his reign was legal definition. His fellow rulers, St Louis, Frederick II and Alfonso the Wise, had all been busy framing laws and constitutions, and Edward, a man of his time, was no exception.

'The laws and customs of the realm'

Edward's great statutes, most of which were enacted in the first half of his reign, were on the whole conservative in tone, merely consolidating principles which were rooted in a much more distant past – the 'laws and customs of the realm'. His aim was to group together and codify the legal system which had grown up in a disorderly fashion in previous generations. His well-known title of the English Justinian had a certain justification: like the famous Byzantine Emperor who codified the Roman law, Edward stood at the end of a long period of legal development and his aim was to arrange and systematise what had gone before him.

On Edward's return from Crusade in 1274 he appointed as Chancellor Robert Burnell, Bishop of Bath and Wells. Burnell was Edward's indispensable servant for the next eighteen years, during which period there was an outburst of legislative activity that was not to be paralleled for centuries. Burnell was a man of modest birth from Acton Burnell in Shropshire; through ability and ambition he came to be one of the senior king's clerks, that select group of clerical technocrats in the royal administration. At every step in his achievements as legislator, administrator and conqueror, Edward had Burnell at his side.

Their first action was to start an inquest into local government: this was to be the starting point of all the later legislation. Commissioners, armed with a list of forty questions, went from county to county asking questions, the answers to which were entered into documents called the Hundred Rolls. They were questions dear to Edward's orderly mind and to his strongly developed sense of royal ownership. Their original purpose was to define royal rights and possessions: the number of the King's manors, which had been sold to religious orders, the encroachments on his rights by his tenants-in-chief, etc.; but the inquiry soon turned into an investigation of local incompetence, corruption and crime. In defining and protecting his own rights, Edward was also acting in the interests of his humbler subjects. The Hundred Rolls may be described as a

The ruins of Acton Burnell Castle in Shropshire, built for Robert Burnell, Bishop of Bath and Wells (1275–92) and Chancellor of England.

thirteenth-century Domesday Book, for they record the legal, economic and social structure of the country at the beginning of Edward's reign.

From the first Parliament of Edward's reign which assembled in April 1275 there emerged the First Statute of Westminster; this dealt with the administrative abuses revealed by the recent commission. Many of its fifty-one laws or chapters were founded in the Great Charter or Magna Carta of 1215. They were essentially a codification of existing laws covering a remarkable number of matters: extortion by royal officers, lawyers, purveyors, bailiffs, etc.; writs and methods of procedure in civil and criminal cases; the custom of wreck; freedom of elections, and many other things besides. In this statute Edward showed his intense dislike of what were variously called liberties, franchises or appurtenances. He disliked them on principle because they formed exceptions to administrative uniformity, and in practice because they protected offenders against the King's peace:

> Because the peace of the land has been weakly kept until now for lack of good pursuit being made of felons and especially because of liberties where felons are received, all shall now be ready and apparelled, at the command of the sheriffs and at the cry of the countryside, to pursue and arrest felons when need arises, within liberties as well as without.

The statute, written in Norman French, was said to be made by the King, 'by his council and by the assent of Archbishops, Bishops, Abbots, Priors, Earls, Barons, and the Community of the Realm being thither summoned'. The secular and 'democratic' introduction to the act may be compared to the pious and aristocratic enactments of Henry's reign, which began with lengthy references to the 'holy and indivisible Trinity . . . the glorious and pre-eminent Mother of God . . . the supreme Pontiff of the Universal Church', and which restricted the King's counsellors to bishops, barons and the 'leading men of England'.

At this Parliament wool was, for the first time, made the

The Wool Trade

Wool was England's most important commodity in the Middle Ages. Most of it was exported to Flanders where it was woven into cloth and then re-exported. The returns from customs on wool represented a large part of the Crown's income.

BELOW Sheep-shearing.
BOTTOM The pastoral scene above the picture of hell in this contemporary manuscript shows shepherds and women weaving.

TOP Merchants waiting for cargoes to arrive in port. ABOVE The dye seal of Winchester which was used for the delivery of wool in the reign of Edward I.

domib[us] hoib[us] nec de aliquib[us] que ad ten[ementa] que h[ab]ent ad firmam spectant nisi sp[eci]ale[m] hu[er]int
concessionem p[er] scripturam sive conventionis mencionem facientem q[uo]d hoc facere possint & si fe-
cerint & sup[er] hoc convincant[ur] dampna plene resarciant & grav[ite]r p[er] m[isericordi]am puniant[ur]. ffirmarii.

Justic' itinerantes de cet[er]o non amercient villatas in itinere suo eo q[uo]d singuli .xii. — xxiiii.
annorum non venerint coram vic' & coronatorib[us] ad inquisitiones de robia & incendio vel aliis
ad coronam spectantib[us] faciend[as] dum tamen de villatis illis veniant sufficientes p[er] quos
hu[jus]modi inquisitiones plene fieri possint except[is] inquisitionib[us] de morte ho[m]i[n]is faciend[is]
ubi omnes .xii. annor[um] venire debent nisi r[aci]onabilem causam h[ab]eant absentie sue. Mur- — xxv.
drum de cet[er]o non adjudicet[ur] coram Justic' ubi infortunium tantummodo adjudicatu[m] est set
locum h[ab]eat murdrum in interfectis p[er] feloniam & non alit[er].

Provisum est eciam q[uo]d — xxvi.
nullus coram Justic' itinerantib[us] occasionetur ad warantu[m] in pl[ac]ito t[er]re audiend[o] p[ro] eo q[uo]d non est p[re]sens
quando vocat[ur] ad warantu[m] excepto primo die in adventu Justic' set si warantus ille fuerit
infra com[itatum] injungat[ur] vic' q[uo]d eum sum[m]oneat infra t[er]ciu[m] diem vel quartum s[e]c[un]d[u]m locor[um] distanciam sic' fieri solebat in itine[re] Justic' fieri consueuit et si ext[r]a com[itatum] maneat tunc r[aci]onabilem h[ab]eat sum-
monicionem .xv. dier[um] ad min[us] s[e]c[un]d[u]m discrecionem Justic' & legem com[mun]em.

Si Cl[er]icus aliquis p[ro] cri- — xxvii.
mine aliquo vel recto quod ad Coronam p[er]tineat arrestatus fu[er]it & postmodum de p[re]cepto
Reg[is] in ballium traditus vel replegiatus extiterit ita q[uo]d hii quib[us] traditus fuit in ballium eu[m] ha-
beant coram Justic' non amercient[ur] illi de cet[er]o quib[us] traditus fuit in ballium vel alii plegii sui si
corpus suu[m] h[ab]eant coram Justic' licet coram eis p[ro]pt[er] p[ri]vilegiu[m] cl[er]icale respondere noluit vel non
possit.

Provisum est eciam q[uo]d si depredaciones vel rapine aliq[ue] fiant abb[at]ib[us] vel aliis — xxviii.
p[re]latis eccl[es]iasticis & ipi o[bier]int de hu[jus]modi depredacoib[us] subsequente morte p[re]venerint an-
tequ[am] justiciam inde fuerint assecuti successores eor[um] h[ab]eant accoem ad bona eccl[es]ie sue de ma-
nib[us] hu[jus]modi transgressor[um] repetend[a]. Similiter eciam h[ab]eant accoem successores de reb[us] que
domui & eccl[es]ie sue fuerint ablate ante obitum p[re]decessor[um] suor[um] si p[er] hu[jus]modi violenciam fuerit subsecuta licet p[re]d[ic]ti p[re]decessores sui inde assecuti non fuerint in vita sua. Si autem in t[em]p[or]e
& ten[ementis] hu[jus]modi religiosor[um] de quib[us] eor[um] p[re]lati obierint deicit ut de ante eccl[es]ie sue aliqui
deforciaverint tempore vacacionis eor[um] successores sui h[ab]eant ad recup[er]and[am] seisinam & advo-
cacionem et dampna sua sicut in nova disseisina adjudicari consueverint. Provisum est eciam
q[uo]d si alienaciones ille de quib[us] b[re]ve de ingressu dari consuevit p[er] tot gradus fiant p[er] quod b[re]ve illud
in forma prius usitata fieri non possit h[ab]eant conquerentes b[re]ve de recup[er]and[a] seisina sine men-
cione graduum ad cujuscumq[ue] manus p[er] hu[jus]modi alienaciones res illa devenerit p[er] b[re]via origi-
nalia p[er] co[mmun]e consiliu[m] d[omi]ni Regis p[ro]videnda.

Explicit statutum de Marlebr' Incipit statutu[m] Westm' primu[m]

Ces sount les establissementz le Roi Edward fitz le Roi Henry fet a son p[ar]lement general
primer ap[re]s son coronement a Westmonster lendemayn de la close de Pasche lan de son
reigne tierz p[ar] son Counseil & p[ar] assentement des Ercheuesques Euesques Abbes
Priours Countes Barons & la comunalte de la t[er]re illeosq[ue]s assemblez. Pur ceo q[ue] n[ost]re
s[eigno]r le Roi ad g[ra]und volunte & desire del estate de son Roialme redresser en les choses ou mestier
est damendement & ceo p[ur] la co[mun]e p[ro]fit de seinte Esglise & du Roialme. Et p[ur] ceo q[ue] lestate de seint
Esglise ad este avant ces houres malement gardez & les p[re]latz & religions de la t[er]re ount

subject of a legislative enactment. Wool was to England what wine was to Gascony: it was the country's most important commodity. Most of the wool was exported to Flanders where the Flemings turned it to cloth which was re-exported. The export duties on wool were payable at London and thirteen other ports, and were collected chiefly by foreign merchants such as Luke of Lucca. Edward was given, 'at the request of the community of merchants', a grant of the customs on exported wool, woolfells and hides. The fact that the merchants requested the imposition of customs showed that some sort of contractual relationship was developing between them and the Crown. The returns from the custom on wool came to nearly £10,000 a year, which represented a large part of the Crown's income.

The first Parliament forbade Jews to practise usury, ordering them to live by merchandise instead. The medieval Jew did not fit into the Christian scheme of things; he therefore had to look for protection to the king, the lord of all men who had no other and the traditional protector of the merchant and foreigner. Most English Jews hailed from France and Germany, but some came from Spain, Italy, and even from Russia and the Moslem countries. They had lived in England in comparative tranquillity until the rising tide of Crusading enthusiasm. During Richard I's coronation celebrations of 1189 the Jewish quarter of York was sacked and its inhabitants massacred. This example was followed throughout the country. Henry III, after extorting all he could from the Jews, mortgaged them to his brother, Richard of Cornwall. With the outbreak of the Baron's War there was a recrudescence of massacres all over the land.

By the time that Edward came to the throne the Jews were so impoverished that their importance to the royal treasury was negligible. As financiers they had been superseded by the Italian merchants. Before that they had been able, being unaffected by the prohibitions on usury, to lend money to church- and castle-builders, Crusaders and tax-payers, enjoying all the time the protection of the king who shared in their gain. Edward's

OPPOSITE A later copy of part of the First Statute of Westminster, 1275, the great reforming and defining code of law which remedied the worst abuses of the rights of lords and tenants which had been discovered by the King's commission the previous year.

Jews suffering persecution at the time of their expulsion from England in 1290.

legislation of 1275 was a bold, some might say cynical, attempt to grapple with the Jewish problem. By forbidding them to practise usury, by encouraging them to engage in commerce, handicrafts and agriculture, he hoped perhaps to make them more acceptable to the rest of the community. However, at the same time he made them more prominent by ordaining that 'each Jew after he is seven years old shall wear a distinguishing mark on his outer garment, that is to say two strips of yellow cloth, six inches long and three inches wide'.

Edward proved unable to stop the Jews practising usury which they now carried on in a clandestine manner. In 1278 they were accused of clipping the coinage; six hundred Jews were arrested for this offence and three hundred were hanged in London in April 1279. In July 1290 Edward expelled all Jews, about 16,160 people, from the country; the measure was highly popular and a grateful Parliament voted him a substantial grant in aid. This measure was, to some modern eyes at least, the greatest crime of Edward's reign.

The ubiquity of the Italian bankers and merchants towards the end of the thirteenth century dealt a final blow to the

OPPOSITE A drawing of the king in profile, with the arms of England on his chest, carrying a staff with a bird on the top. It comes from the Memorandum Roll, one of the records of royal administration, dating from 1297–8.

Treuge communia

De ulter' treug' alius assign' ad articulos suffe rencie guerre int' rege Angl' & rege Ffrancie custodiend'

Edward par la grace de
A ceux qe ces lettres ve
e [illegible] entre nous por no
e le Roi de Ffraunce p
part e nos les descend
e aidaunz dune part e
dautre. La quelle suf
e dilueqes iusqes a
emendrons e ferons e
chescun des noz homm
abstinence de suffrance
[illegible] aucunes person

eminence of the Jews as money-lenders. Boniface VIII had skilfully brought over the Italian merchants – the Frescobaldi, Bardi, Pozzi and others – in Florence and other cities to his side. That he could do this was a result of the immense attention given to the reorganisation and clarification of the Church's finances throughout Europe since the pontificate of Innocent III. It was now illegal for the Church's revenues to be put to secular uses, unless papal permission had previously been obtained. The papacy obtained a vast revenue from western Europe by way of taxation, judicial fees and the income from benefices. The merchants of Florence transmitted these revenues often in the form of wool or cloth, and credited the papacy with the values. In 1252 Florence had acquired a further financial strength by minting the gold florin which soon became the standard currency in the west and the easiest way of making large payments in cash: in short, the Florentines now controlled the money market. Edward had desperate need of the Italian bankers and it was partly to please them as well as his own subjects, not to mention his fiercely anti-Semitic wife and mother, that he expelled the Jews from England. The country became the hunting-ground of Italian merchant bankers because of England's monopoly of the wool trade and because of Edward's permanent need of money to finance his wars.

The Statute of Gloucester of 1278 was the next landmark in Edward's legal reforms. This attempt to define and regulate the special franchises of the feudal barons was followed up by the Statute of *Quo Warranto* in 1290. Edward's orderly mind was disturbed by the way in which the great immunities of the feudal lords broke up the uniform administration of justice. He regarded the feudal jurisdictions as dangerous to the authority of the Crown as well as being obstacles to a cheap and efficient system of justice for all the people. Justices were sent out all over the country to inquire into the rights or warrants of feudal magnates to administer the law by their own courts, i.e. the grounds on which they claimed their franchises. 'We must find out what is ours, and is due to us, and others, what is theirs and what is due to them.' The assumption of the statute was that every liberty belonged to the Crown unless the holder of it had sufficient warrant by charter and from time immemorial. (For this purpose, 'time immemorial' was deemed to date from the coronation of Richard I in 1189.) Many magnates reacted angrily to the interrogation, regarding it as a high-handed piece of royal blackmail.

The Statute of Mortmain in 1279 forbade gifts of land to be made to the Church without royal licence. This was another seemingly peremptory piece of legislation; henceforward, whenever a gift of property was made to the Church, the King received a licence fee. It has been suggested that this was Edward's way of showing disapproval of the Archbishop of Canterbury's (John Peckham's) instruction that a new copy of Magna Carta be nailed up annually in every major church. In fact, it was a justifiable step to put an end to a prevalent abuse whereby estates could be conveyed to religious foundations, thus evading death duties; the donor then held them as fiefs of the Church. 'The services which are due from such fees for the defence of the realm are unjustifiably withdrawn.'

ABOVE A silver groat, with a bust of King Edward, minted in London, 1279–80.
BELOW Reverse of the same coin, decorated with a long cross.

In 1285 the Statute of Winchester codified and strengthened the police system for preserving public order ('robberies, murders and arsons are more often committed than they used to be'), while in the same year the Second Statute of Westminster, usually referred to as *De Donis Conditionalibus*, became the foundation of estates tail, restricting the alienation of land. This momentous statute affected the whole future land law of England. The new hereditable estates created by the act were called estates tail because they were 'cut off' (*taillé*) from the fee. A tenant was only a tenant for life and had no power of alienating the estate. The act showed the influence of the nobles as they, as well as the King, stood to gain from the increased chances of reversion. It also stated that 'the will of the donor manifestly expressed in the charter of the gift is to be observed henceforth'; until then the recipient had been able to alienate gifts of land, thus frustrating the intention of the donor. The result of this statute was to keep entailed estates within the family circle until the present day.

Finally, in 1290, the Third Statute of Westminster, known as *Quia Emptores*, dealt with land held not upon condition but in fee simple. Land acquired in this way could be freely alienated, but in future the new owner held his land from the lord of the seller by the same services and customs as were attached to it before the sale. Thus it called a halt to sub-infeudation, once again increasing the power and wealth of the King and nobles. This was the last piece of constructive legislation in Edward's reign.

Historians will discuss indefinitely whether a date can be set to mark the end of feudalism. Certainly *Quia Emptores* cut at the root of the feudal principle, as the constant creation of new links of feudal service was an essential part of the system. The early fourteenth century saw the appearance of 'bastard feudalism', that is the replacement of homage by patronage. Henceforward troops were recruited for money and no longer as a part of the feudal obligation. Elements of feudalism, however, survived until the end of the fifteenth century.

Edward's personal piety and unblemished orthodoxy did not prevent him from having his fair share of trouble with the papacy and the English Church. The thirteenth century witnessed an astonishing growth both of papal pretensions and

Scenes of country life in early fourteenth-century England.

ABOVE A manuscript illustration of a cart and horse.

OPPOSITE Farmers reaping and harvesting from the Luttrell Psalter.

LEFT An illustration from a medieval calendar of a farmer and his animals at market.

also of national power, and it was inevitable that the two would come into conflict. If it was difficult to define royal relations with the papacy, it was harder still to define the relations between the Crown and the national Church. There were at the best of times plenty of opportunities for trouble where two different systems of law prevailed side by side, one for the layman and one for the clergy, with uncertain and overlapping jurisdictions; where bishops and clergy suffered under the incubus of a double allegiance, to the pope and to the king. Edward's attitude was that priests as well as laymen should submit themselves to the King, who was as much the Lord's Anointed as a bishop or abbot. Like the lords of a feudal franchise, the clergy might rule within their own sphere, but Edward saw to it that the sphere was defined as narrowly as possible.

A friend of popes and cardinals

In spite of disputes about taxation, privileges and jurisdiction, Edward's reign was not on the whole a time of serious friction between Church and State. He was a devout man, a Crusader, at ease with monks and clergy, a friend of popes and cardinals, and loyal to the Church and its system of government, except when his will was thwarted. On the other hand he had a livelier sense of what was due to Caesar than his father, who sometimes gave the impression that he derived pious satisfaction from his ostentatious subservience to the papal will. A passion for legal definition, chronic shortage of money, a belief that the anointed king was the patron and protector of the clergy: all these considerations coloured Edward's attitude to ecclesiastical authority.

John Peckham, a Franciscan friar, was Archbishop of Canterbury from 1279 to 1292, having succeeded the Dominican Robert Kilwardby. Peckham (or Pecham) has gone down in history as an amiable fusspot; he was a good friend to Edward and the royal family and an efficient administrator of his vast province in England and Wales. Although, as a Franciscan, he attached great importance to his pastoral duties, he also held strong views about the rights of the Church and, on one occasion, took a firm line in resisting what he considered to be lay interference in ecclesiastical liberties. Shortly after he became Archbishop, in 1279, he offended the King by making some provocative pronouncements at his first provincial council at Reading. He attacked pluralities (the possession of more than one benefice), which were the Crown's principal method of supplementing the incomes of civil servants. He announced sentences of excommunication against various classes of persons: those who tried to prevent an ecclesiastical judge from trying cases which belonged to canon law; those of the King's ministers who disobeyed the royal writ requiring them to arrest an excommunicated person; and those who violated Magna Carta.

Edward's answer was a counter-offensive in the form of the Statute of Mortmain and a summons to Peckham to appear before the King and Council in Parliament, where he was ordered to withdraw the sentence of excommunication and to have removed from church doors the texts of Magna Carta. Edward particularly disliked being reminded of the first chapter of that charter which promised that 'the English Church shall be free, and shall have its rights undiminished and its liberties unimpaired'. Peckham gave way, but followed up his surrender a month later with a letter to the King. In it he wrote, 'By no human constitution, not even by an oath, can we be bound to ignore laws which rest undoubtedly on divine authority.'

'The English Church shall be free'

The worst dispute between King and Church occurred in August 1297, almost twenty years later. Peckham had died in 1292 and was succeeded as Archbishop of Canterbury by Robert Winchelsey (or Winchelsea), a stubborn, conscientious man who did his best to serve both King and Pope. Edward was facing the biggest crisis of his reign: he found himself entangled in wars in France, Flanders, Scotland, Gascony and Wales; he was in desperate need of money and Parliament was unsympathetic to his requests. The Pope was Boniface VIII who was trying, with pedantic legalism, to maintain the authority of Innocent III at a time when the power of the papacy had become irreparably weakened by the steadily increasing strength of the lay powers. In 1296 Boniface issued his famous bull *Clericis*

Laicos which forbade lay taxation of the clergy without the authority of the Holy See. Whoever disobeyed this bull would be *ipso facto* excommunicated. When Edward demanded a subsidy of a fifth from the clergy for his wars, Winchelsey refused to pay on the grounds that papal authority was needed. Edward thereupon declared the clergy to be outlawed: no longer would they enjoy royal protection, nor would they have redress in the courts for injury or theft. He seized all lay fees held by clerics and warned that ecclesiastical fees would be seized in the same way. Winchelsey retaliated by renewing his threat to excommunicate anyone who should disobey papal decrees. A calmer mood soon prevailed, however, and the Pope, in a new bull, *Etsi de statu*, declared that *Clericis Laicos* did not apply when there was a state of emergency, and that the King could determine what constituted an emergency.

This was one of the incidents towards the end of Edward's reign which was fraught with the issues of arbitrary royal power and English liberty. It opened that unhappy final period known as the 'years of emergency' when all Edward's well-laid plans were clearly going awry. It seemed to Bishop Stubbs that 'every difficulty and embarrassment under which the King laboured serves to enhance the greatness of the man who with such drawbacks on his activity could do so much . . . he was throughout his reign deeply in debt, and in every section of his government, hampered by opposition from the leading prelates of the time'. Stubbs attributed every event of these years, when Edward's behaviour fell far short of what might have been expected of him, to two causes: his chronic indebtedness and various ecclesiastical traditions inherited from his father.

The quarrel between Edward and Winchelsey was the nearest England came in Edward's reign to a repetition of the crisis between Henry II and Thomas Becket. Some say that Winchelsey's stand was in the interests of popular liberty, while others maintain that it was a sullen determination to resist what were necessary measures of strong government. As it was, it coincided with the baronial disapproval of Edward's extravagant and unsuccessful military policies, and this led to the

OPPOSITE A fresco by Giotto, *c.* 1300, of Boniface VIII, whose famous bull, *Unam Sanctam* – the most absolute proclamation of papal authority – led to Philip IV's extreme reaction, the 'Outrage of Anagni', when his troops forced their way into the Pope's palace and tried o abduct him.

OVERLEAF LEFT The Court of Common Pleas, from *The Whaddon Folio, c.* 1460. This court sat permanently in Westminster Hall to adjudicate, with the help of local juries from the shires, disputes between the owners of freehold land. Edward emphasised the importance of continuity in the administration of justice by encouraging the growth of the existing courts of law, particularly the Court of Common Pleas, the King's Bench and the Court of the Exchequer.

OVERLEAF RIGHT Edward I in Parliament, from the manuscript of Sir Thomas Wriothesley who died in 1534. On the left of the King is Alexander III of Scotland, on the right Llewelyn ap Gruffydd of Wales.

Acompt
Addicion
Administrators
Age
Aied
Aied de roy
Accions sur lestat
Accions sur le cas
Admesurement
Amerciements

Annuite
Arbitrement
Assise
Assigne
Attachement
Attaint
Attornay
Attornement
Auncien demesne
Audita querela

longtain voyage : quil souffira de porter seulemet vng
las de soye a vng ymage de sainct george pendāt a icelluj.
Aussi se ledit colier dor auoit besoing de reparacion il pōra
estre mis en la main de louurier iusques a ce quil soit
repare. Lequel colier aussi ne pourra estre enrichy de
pierres ou daultres choses reserue led ymage qui pourra
estre garny au plaisir du cheualier. Et aussi ne pourra
estre ledit colier vendu engaige donne ne aliene pour
necessite ou cause quelconque que ce soit

Sacred
to the memory of
JAMES BERNARD RUCK

formidable combination of secular and ecclesiastical opposition which was too strong for him. In 1297 he was forced to confirm the Charters (Magna Carta and the Charter of the Forest), and in 1301 he suffered at Lincoln an humiliation at the hands of Winchelsey which he never forgave. Winchelsey refused him any money from the Church until the perambulation of the forests had been enforced. Perambulation meant, in effect, a restriction of the King's prerogative rights in the forests and a corresponding diminution in his income from them. Edward had therefore to rely on his income from other sources such as the Church. He took his revenge on Winchelsey when the Scots were apparently subdued. When his own Gascon subject, Betrant Got, became Pope as Clement V in 1305, he sent his trusted minister Walter de Langton, Bishop of Coventry and Lichfield, to Rome with the object of discrediting Winchelsey. Langton had earlier been charged, with Winchelsey's connivance, with adultery, concubinage, simony and intercourse with the devil. He took therefore a certain gleeful delight in fulfilling his mission. Winchelsey was suspended by the Pope and left England, not to return until the following reign.

OPPOSITE The ruins of the north transept of the church at Winchelsea, founded by Edward I as part of the new town he ordered to be built after the old town was almost totally destroyed by flooding. Robert of Winchelsey, Archbishop of Canterbury from 1292 to 1306, was probably born in the old town.

6 Edward and Europ

1274-1307

PREVIOUS PAGES Edward I returning from Gascony, from an early fifteenth-century manuscript.

EDWARD WAS BY BIRTH and temperament a European and he took an intense interest in everything that happened on the Continent. After returning to England as King in 1274, he kept in constant touch with the Continent through alliances – military and matrimonial – and through the affairs of his distant duchy, Gascony. In 1286 he went to the duchy and stayed for three years. During this time he displayed, as usual, his prodigious mental and physical energy by travelling indefatigably from place to place, supervising every branch of the administration, dispensing justice and settling disputes. He conciliated the nobles, protected the merchants, encouraged trade, put down disorder by strengthening the fortifications of existing towns and by building new fortified towns or *bastides*. He brought with him from England his Chancellor, Burnell, half his Council and half his Chancery. His Wardrobe, with its Treasurer acting as a sort of 'travelling banker', provided for his heavy expenditure and audited the accounts of his local officials. Edward did his best to turn the administratively chaotic duchy, with its lawless feuding nobility, into a model colony contentedly enjoying the blessings of his enlightened rule.

Few rulers stood higher in general esteem than Edward did. He was acclaimed as a Crusader and sought as an arbitrator. He came as near as anyone toward filling the gap left in European politics by the death of St Louis. Edward did not, of course, have the charm or holiness of character of that great King; he was a conventional man in an age of change. With Louis' death, gone were the rulers with a universal vision, with the nation states subordinating their local interests to those of western Christendom as a whole, taking their lead from a strong papacy. Gone also, with the death of Frederick II in 1250, were the German emperors with their own vision of the imperial power as the unifying principle of an harmonious society of kingdoms and cities. It has been said that the late thirteenth century was the age of the *regnum* (kingdom), not of the *imperium* (empire).

OPPOSITE Edward I pays homage to Philip IV, the Fair, in 1286, from the *Grandes Chroniques de France* by Jean Fouquet.

Edward's great adversary on the Continent was his cousin, Philip IV (the Fair) of France, who ruled from 1285 to 1314. Henry III's treaty with St Louis in 1259 (the Treaty of Paris) had

Boniface VIII presides over his consistory, from a late fourteenth-century manuscript of his *Liber Sextus*.

had a remarkably stabilising effect on Anglo-French relations: it led to a period of peace between the two countries which lasted for thirty years. During these years, however, national attitudes were hardening fast. France, under her able rulers, was becoming the most powerful country in Europe. As the papacy declined, the French monarchy consolidated its power, each expansionist territorial act being justified by a group of clever lawyers and ministers with fanatical belief in the theory of royal autocracy. The years before and after the turn of the century were characterised by the life-and-death struggle between the papacy and not, as one might have expected, the German Empire, but France.

The pontificate of Boniface VIII (1294–1303) exemplified the

The crowning of Philip III of France who ruled from 1270 to 1285 and laid the way for his son's (Philip the Fair) impressive position of power by great acquisitions of territory in France.

great question of the later Middle Ages: could papal authority exercise in practice the theory of papal sovereignty over Christendom? The more often Philip the Fair belaboured the Church with increasing cynicism and brutality, the more absolute grew the claims of Boniface VIII, culminating in 1302 with his great bull *Unam Sanctam*, the most absolute proclamation of theocratic doctrine ever formulated in the Middle Ages. It ended with the words, 'We declare, say, define and pronounce that it is a necessity of salvation for every human creature to be subject to the Roman pontiff.' Philip IV's violent answer to this was the 'Outrage of Anagni' in September 1303, when his troops forced their way into the Pope's palace and tried to abduct him. Although they failed, the Pope died of

The reverse of the gold seal of Ludwig of Bavaria shows Rome in 1328. The papacy in the Middle Ages insisted on its total sovereignty over Christendom which caused major disputes between Church and State.

shock a short while later. Accusations against Boniface proved useful in Philip's dealings with his successor, Benedict XI, and even more so with Clement V who transferred the papal Curia from Rome to Avignon to please the French King. During the years of the 'Babylonian Captivity' at Avignon (1309–77), the papacy was widely, if unjustly, regarded as a tool of French policy.

Philip the Fair and his lawyers tried similar strong-arm tactics against Edward in respect of his French possessions. Edward was repelled by the fanaticism which possessed the legists of the French King; it made his own pedantic insistence on his legal rights look naïve by comparison. Edward was duped by Philip in the same way that John Balliol was duped by Edward. Indeed, the only people who could outwit Edward were the French King and his able lawyers. Edward's difficulty was that he recognised that his vassal status carried with it certain obligations towards Philip, in the same way that his own vassals had obligations towards him. Philip the Fair played for all he was worth on the confusion and anomalies inherent in this situation. To be a sovereign and a vassal at the same time was a difficult matter.

King Philip the Fair was handsome, reserved, formally devout and a lover of sport. Unlike Edward, he was not a hard worker. He picked with care his able, flint-hearted bureaucrats, to whom kingship was the first article of faith. From this charmed circle he chose his evil ministers – Guillaume de Nogaret, for example, who master-minded the campaign against Boniface VIII and, a few years later, the attack on the Knights Templar. Philip's position of power was derived largely from the vast territorial acquisitions of his father, Philip III (the Bold), whose reign (1270–85) is generally thought of as short and colourless. In fact, during those brief years, he acquired the lands of his uncle, the Count of Poitou and Toulouse, the county of Champagne – the richest fief in France – and the little kingdom of Navarre, south of Gascony. Henry, and later Edward, looked on indulgently as Philip III enlarged his dominions. Philip the Fair's breach of faith and his famous

The coronation of Pope Clement v in the presence of Philip iv of France and his brother, Charles of Valois.

coup in Gascony in 1294 are all the more shocking when seen in this light.

Edward has been criticised by historians for failing during those years to throw his weight against the new acquisitive tendencies in French policy. He was, however, doing what he could to help preserve the peace of Europe. He exerted himself to find a solution to the serious disputes between the French royal house and Aragon and Castile. In the Empire he appeared as an arbitrator and managed to settle a quarrel between Brabant and Gelders. Count Philip of Savoy asked Edward and his mother, Eleanor, to decide upon his successor. Of much greater significance in British history was Edward's role as

Seal of the Knights Templar, the great international crusading order whose wealth in France was confiscated by Philip the Fair to fill the Crown's coffers after trumped-up accusations of heresy and black magic.

arbitrator in the question of the Scottish succession when, as we shall see, he imposed through force and cunning his overlordship on Scotland.

The outbreak of war between England and France in 1294 surprised the statesmen of Europe. The new aggressive character of the French monarchy had not been fully appreciated, particularly by Edward. His attitude to his royal European relations was an amiable one. He liked them all and respected the territorial integrity of their various kingdoms. The ruling houses in France, England, Castile, Aragon, Navarre, Sicily and Provence were all closely related to each other. The only serious disturber of the peace was Charles of Anjou, St Louis' unpleasant younger brother. It soon became apparent that he represented a new tradition in the French Court, one that was hostile to all that his brother had stood for. Or perhaps it was rather the revival of an old tradition, a return to the expansionist days of Philip Augustus, who during his reign from 1180 to 1223 destroyed the English-based Angevin Empire and greatly extended the influence of his dynasty. Charles of Anjou pursued a policy of cynicism, unscrupulousness and brutality to further his ends, which were the political expansion of France and a bellicose revival of the pseudo-Carolingian tradition. Philip the Fair shared this new outlook. There was something formidable and frightening in his steely purposefulness and it is difficult not to feel sorry for Edward in his dealings with this ambitious creature. The cruellest and most cynical act of Philip's reign was his attack on the Order of the Knights Templar in 1307. Philip wanted their wealth and their lands and he stopped at nothing to get them. The French Templars were thrown into prison and tortured into admitting crimes such as heresy, idolatry and immorality. Behind a façade of legalism, Philip had these men tortured to death for no other reason than that he wanted their money. This practice of false charges, torture and lying propaganda became a feature of French legal procedure until the Revolution of 1789. Philip also, although in this case he can be said to have been acting in accordance with the spirit of the times, had all the Jews expelled from France in 1306, seizing their property and confiscating all their lands. Again the motive behind this act was the desire to increase the wealth of the French Crown.

Philip the Fair's aggression in Gascony came as a surprise to Edward. What caused his sudden change of policy from peace to war, and why, having made it, did he not pursue the conflict to its logical conclusion? Neither Philip the Fair nor his father had been scrupulous in fulfilling those promises made by St Louis to Henry III in 1259. Several important bishoprics and the lands of Saintonge and the Agenais should have been handed over to the English King. The Agenais linked up Gascony proper with Périgord and commanded the valley of the Garonne. When Edward did homage to Philip III for Gascony in 1273, he did so 'for the lands which I ought to hold of you'. In 1279 the Agenais was finally extracted from the French King, and much of Edward's time, during his long visit to France from 1286 to 1289, was spent receiving homages, creating *bastides* and generally putting order into this rich and important part of his French territories.

When Philip the Fair came to the throne in 1285 he turned out to be a crafty and dangerous overlord. He was angered by the relative independence of Aquitaine under its King-Duke, and embarked at first on a war of nerves, keeping lands which should have been ceded, encouraging appeals to the French Court, and putting French officials in Périgord and other territories not belonging to him. Tension mounted and there was bound, sooner or later, to be a *cause célèbre*. It came in May 1293 when the endemic piracy practised by Breton and Norman sailors on the one hand, and English and Gascon, especially Bayonnais, on the other, turned into something like real war. Some ships from the Cinque Ports (Hastings, Romney, Hythe, Dover and Sandwich) destroyed a Norman fleet off Brittany and the Bayonnais sacked La Rochelle. Philip the Fair immediately used the incident as a pretext for the occupation of Bordeaux, the Agenais and Périgord.

In January 1294 Edward was summoned to Paris as the French King's vassal, 'to answer for these evil deeds and to do justice . . . . Whether you appear or not, we shall proceed against you despite your absence'. Edward sent in his stead his brother, Edmund of Lancaster, whose wife Blanche was the mother-in-law of Philip the Fair. It was agreed that twenty Gascon hostages be given up; that six border towns in the Agenais and Saintonge be temporarily surrendered to France; and that the French King would be allowed to put 'one man or two' into some other towns and fortresses, including Bordeaux and Bayonne. Furthermore, Edward was to marry Philip's sister, Margaret (Queen Eleanor having died in 1290), which he did five years later, and the duchy was to be given in perpetuity to their issue. In return for these arrangements, worked out by Edmund and the three French Queens – the Queen Dowager, Marie of Brabant, Philip's wife Jeanne, and her mother Blanche, the wife of Edmund and Dowager Queen of Navarre – Philip would return the duchy to Edward within forty days, repeal the summons that Edward appear in Paris as a disobedient vassal, and issue him with a safe conduct to come to Amiens to ratify the agreement.

What went wrong? Edward 'in all simplicity' fulfilled the terms of this secret treaty: the towns and hostages were delivered and warlike preparations abandoned. Philip, however, sent not 'one man or two' into Gascony but, in the words of a chronicler, 'first a few, then many, then an army'. He refused Edward a safe conduct, proclaimed him a contumacious vassal in May 1294, and declared that the whole fief was forfeited to the French King. Edward was condemned as a defaulter and the duchy was confiscated. This then was Philip's famous *coup* of 1294.

Edward, although stunned and outraged, did not waste time in blaming his unfortunate brother, who returned sorrowfully to England declaring himself to be 'a fool or as one seduced'. He at once prepared for the reconquest of his lost duchy. His English subjects were generally less affected than their ruler by the news from Gascony: for them it was a distant and irrelevant possession for which they were always being taxed. However, on this occasion they shared Edward's indignation at the

The Kingdom of France 1274-1314
HOLLAND
London
R. Thames
Winchester
Dover
Winchelsea
Hastings
Portsmouth
FLANDERS
Ghent
BRABANT
Boulogne
Courtrai
Montreuil-sur-Mer
ARTOIS
HAINAULT
English Channel
PONTHIEU
Amiens
THE EMPIRE
R. Seine
NORMANDY
CHAMPAGNE
Paris
BRITTANY
MAINE
BURGUNDY
ANJOU
R. Loire
BLOIS
TOURAINE
POITOU
DUCHY OF
AQUITAINE
Châlons
La Rochelle
LA MARCHE
SAINTONGE
Angoulême
AUVERGNE
R. Rhône
Blaye
Bourg
PÉRIGORD
R. Dordogne
Bordeaux
Libourne
AGENAIS
R. Lot
Marmande
Agen
PROVENCE
Avignon
GASCONY
Arles
Bayonne
Marseilles
SOULE
BÉARN
BIGORRE
R. Garonne
CASTILE
Burgos
NAVARRE
Acquisitions of Philip III and Philip IV 1270-1314
English territory in 1314
Scale 0 50 100 150 miles

behaviour of Philip, and Parliament assented to a series of drastic and arbitrary measures for raising money. This was the last time in his reign that Edward was to be allowed to 'get away' with such things. He seized all the wool, hides and fells in England, and also the money from the abbeys and priories which had been collected for his Crusade. These actions were to lead to political trouble later. An army was assembled at Portsmouth, ready to embark when, in September 1294, Wales broke out in revolt and Edward marched west with a great part of the army intended for Gascony. This was an example of Edward's tendency to get militarily involved on different fronts at the same time. He had neither the skill nor the resources to fight simultaneous wars, and the only one which can be called successful was the war in Wales which he won, not by any brilliant strategy, but by pouring vast resources into that tiny country.

The reconquest of Gascony proceeded ingloriously. The remains of the army at Portsmouth sailed to Gascony under the command of Edward's nephew, John of Brittany, in October 1294, to be followed a couple of months later by another expedition under Edmund of Lancaster and the Earl of Lincoln. The English captured Bourg and Blaye in the north, the key towns for the control of the Gironde, and also Bayonne in the south. On the other hand, the French armies under Charles of Valois, Philip's brother, and Robert of Artois, the brother-in-law of his adversary in the field, Edmund of Lancaster, were more than holding their ground. Charles of Valois was thought to have egged his brother Philip on to break his word with Edward over Gascony. The English were unable to consolidate their position outside their strongholds in the north and south, and they could not dislodge the French from Bordeaux.

In the summer of 1296, Edmund died at Bayonne. This loyal younger brother of the King, estimable as he was, does not appear to have had a very forceful personality; loyalty, decency, modesty and piety were his excellent virtues. He was only nine years old when his father accepted on his behalf the Sicilian throne, so we can assume that his own wishes played little part in the decision. He was said to have been very disappointed when the barons later insisted that Henry revoke his acceptance. A crown having eluded him, Edmund decided instead to accumulate riches for himself. After the Battle of Evesham, he urged Henry to carry out sweeping measures of confiscation of the rebels' property, hoping that much of it would come his way – which it did. On Simon de Montfort's death, Edmund was created Earl of Leicester. He commanded a division of the royal army at Kenilworth, and when the castle surrendered, Henry gave it to him. Although Edmund was six years younger than Edward, the rumour was spread in the following century, by John of Gaunt and others, that Edmund was Henry's deformed elder son who had been passed over as unfit to rule. His nickname of 'Crouchback' might have had something to do with this, although it was in fact another way of saying 'Crossed Back' which the Londoners called him when he returned from Edward's Crusade in 1272, having accomplished there little or nothing. Edmund's loyalty to his brother made him a perfect 'trouble-shooter' for the King, even if he was at times lacking in energy and judgment. After his marriage to Blanche of Artois, widow of the Count of Champagne and King of Navarre, Edmund took the title of Count of Champagne and Brie. He was England's greatest landowner, with holdings in twenty-five shires and throughout south Wales. He was, by all accounts, religious, cheerful, open-handed and popular with all.

After Edmund's death, the Earl of Lincoln lost the only encounter with the French which approached the status of a battle in the inconclusive war in Gascony. For military historians the conflict hardly deserves to be called a war: there were no memorable battles or sieges, and many examples of incompetence. Even after the Welsh revolt had been subdued, Edward did not go in person to Gascony. He preferred to play at the diplomatic power game in the Rhineland and the Low Countries, and to make alliances in Germany and Flanders. The purpose was to weaken Philip by getting him to divert his troops from Gascony to north-eastern France, and thus to fight on two fronts – a familiar situation for Edward. This meant, of course, another English army in Flanders and the further diminution of a collective English military effort.

Edward used trusted emissaries like Amadeus of Savoy and Otto de Grandison, who travelled the length of the French frontier, from the mouth of the Rhine to as far south as Savoy and Burgundy. They discussed alliances and handed out sums of money, large and small, depending on the importance of the recipient. Otto de Grandison was one of Edward's closest friends and at the centre of every important event throughout the reign. The two men may originally have met in Savoy. The castle of Grandson, near Neuchâtel, on the confines of Savoyard and Habsburg territory, was one of those castles whose traits were reproduced in the Edwardian castles of north Wales. Otto himself may have employed Master James of St George at Grandson. Before being entrusted by Edward with important diplomatic missions, he had held high military commands in Wales and was constable of Caernarvon Castle.

Edward's policy of concluding treaties of friendship in Germany and the Low Countries was not a new one. In 1277 a marriage had been arranged between his daughter, Joan of Acre, and Hartmann, son of Rudolf of Habsburg, King of the Romans, and founder, to all intents and purposes, of the Imperial House of Habsburg, which, with its capital at Vienna, was to dominate central European politics on and off for the next six

The seal of Rudolf of Habsburg, King of the Romans and founder of the Imperial House of Habsburg. Edward I's alliance with Rudolf and Germany was important to England in balancing the growing power of the King of France and Charles of Anjon.

hundred years. Rudolf was one of the most popular princes of his day and, with him as Emperor-elect, there was a reasonable chance that some of the authority and dignity of the Empire would be restored. Although he was a much more affable, attractive character than Edward, both were the subject of many admiring contemporary anecdotes on account of their knightly qualities. The marriage between Joan and Hartmann, however, never materialised: he was drowned in the Rhine near Strasbourg in 1277.

At this point, and for a long time to come, Germany and England represented two opposite extremes in the development of the State: one unified and centralised, and the other consisting of thousands of independent and semi-independent principalities, duchies and cities. Edward furthered the monarchical tendencies of English society by the exploitation of the royal prerogative, while German society remained essentially feudal.

Edward saw his alliance with Rudolf as balancing, in some measure, the growing power of the King of France and Charles of Anjou. He was well aware of the limited authority and effectiveness of Rudolf of Habsburg, or indeed of any emperor-elect. The pitiful achievements of his uncle Richard of Cornwall's reign as King of the Romans were a sufficient reminder of the contrast between the claims and realities of this high office. Such an alliance would, thought Edward, be of psychological advantage with the rulers of the states in the Low Countries: Flanders, Brabant, Cleves, Gelders and Holland. Marriages were accordingly arranged, some of which took place, between his son, Edward of Caernarvon, and Philippa, daughter of Guy, Count of Flanders, and between Edward's daughters, Margaret, Eleanor and Elizabeth, with the Duke of Brabant and the Counts of Bar and Holland. At Nuremberg in 1294 a grand alliance was formed between Edward, these rulers and Adolf of Nassau, the new Emperor-elect, Rudolf of Habsburg having died in 1291.

The alliance of Edward and the Rhineland princes was weakened by the defection of the Count of Holland and Adolf

Edward I (left) confronting Philip IV of France in 1297, from a sketch on an Exchequer Memorandum Roll.

of Nassau, who had probably been bribed by Philip not to intervene in Flanders. Boniface VIII now offered his services as arbitrator in his private capacity as Benedict Gaetani. These were, in the end, welcome to Edward and Philip. Edward was facing the biggest crisis of his reign with his rebellious barons and bishops and he had been forced, at his Continental headquarters at Ghent, to surrender to their demands. In 1299 he reached an understanding with Philip at Montreuil-sur-Mer near Boulogne, thereby leaving his ally, the Count of Flanders, in the lurch and earning for himself the title of *perfidus anglorum rex* in the Flemish chronicles. Three years later, in July 1303, Philip was overwhelmingly defeated by the Flemings at Courtrai (or Kortrijk), which prevented for all time the absorption of Flanders into France. In 1303 a definite peace treaty was made between England and France, under which

Philip restored the duchy of Gascony in its entirety to Edward, and the kings of England remained vassals of the kings of France. The French continued to resent the fact that this rich and beautiful duchy, culturally and geographically a part of France, did not belong to them, and they never accepted the situation. Nevertheless, Gascony, England's first colony, remained English for the next one and a half centuries until it surrendered to the French in 1453, the year of the fall of Constantinople.

Edward's European activities, with their undramatic and inconclusive outcome, now seem to have little historical significance, but there is one activity for which he deserves to be remembered on the Continent, as well as in Britain, and that is as a builder of new fortified towns or *bastides*. The first *bastide* in Gascony, the Marmande on the Garonne, was founded by Richard I in 1182. After that little was done in the area until the middle of the thirteenth century when dozens of *bastides* were founded in quick succession in the Agenais by Alphonse de Poitiers, Lord of Toulouse and younger brother of St Louis. The Agenais, which had been given by Richard I to his sister Joan as her dowry in 1196, reverted to the duchy of Aquitaine, as stipulated in the Treaty of Paris, when the Count of Toulouse and his wife both died childless in 1271.

Nearly 140 *bastides* were founded in Gascony during Edward's reign. He took a great interest in these foundations for their purpose was to increase his revenues and his political power within the duchy. Edward had very few estates of his own in Gascony and his economic and political strength lay in how far he could exploit his position as the feudal overlord. One of the advantages of *bastides* was that they scattered the duchy with communities that were loyal to Edward, and the merchants and traders residing within them could always be called on to provide him with loans.

Edward had a special instrument to found *bastides* in Gascony on sites that did not lie on his demesnes: this was the partnership or *paréage*. A local landowner – it could be a baron, a bishop or a monastery – would be taken by Edward into partnership. The landowner provided the site and the royal patron endowed the town with liberties and promised his protection. The revenues from the town were divided among the partners, usually in equal shares. Nearly half the foundations in Gascony were by *paréage*, and three-quarters of these involved the English Crown. When the *bastide* was founded, the event was marked by a ceremony: a pole was erected at the centre of the place where the streets and plots had been marked

The fortified church in the town of Villeréal in the Lot and Garonne region of France. During Edward's reign he founded and built numerous fortified towns or *bastides* in Gascony outside his own demesne with the help of local landowners whom he took into partnership.

out, and a flag was hoisted bearing the emblems of the founders.

The original pattern of the streets and 'blocks' of the *bastides* built by Edward and his partners is much easier to appreciate than those of the new towns which Edward built in England and Wales. The plans were simple and rectangular, like those of American cities which, since a large number of plantations were planned within a short number of years, tended to have similar if not identical internal patterns. The straight parallel streets radiated out from a central square which contained the public buildings. The characteristic features of the *bastide* can still be seen in the rolling hill country between the Dordogne and the Lot; there, little towns like Beaumont and Monpaxier still have a quaint arcaded central square, straight-cut narrow lanes, fortified churches and picturesque houses, walls and gateways, which look much as they did when built at the instigation of their English Duke.

The *bastides* were created both for military reasons, and more importantly to increase the population and further trade. Most of them were not near the frontiers but on good soil rich with economic possibilities. Most had no ramparts and were of no military use. Some of them were founded, or inspired, by English officials who had been posted over there, or by Edward's friends and counsellors. One such trusted official was Roger Leybourne (or Leyburn) who gave his name to Libourne, the most important of Edward's *bastides*. It is situated at the confluence of the Rivers Gironde and Isle, at the highest point to which the wine-ships that traded with England could penetrate from the sea.

It must not be thought that there was anything original in Edward's policy of founding towns in Aquitaine: he was neither the first nor only builder of *bastides*. Both St Louis and Alphonse of Poitiers had been active before him. Edward, however, carried out his work of imitation with such energy and persistence that there was no part of Europe, except perhaps the new towns on the eastern confines of Germany, where *bastides* had such an important and lasting influence as in Gascony.

7 The Great Cause 1290–1307

PREVIOUS PAGES Casts of two seals of John Balliol who was crowned King of Scotland in 1292. Edward regarded Balliol and his country as a feudal vassal under the sovereignty of the realm of England.

DID THE KING OF SCOTS hold his realm as a vassal of the King of England? This was the question which obsessed Edward during the final decade of the thirteenth century. Through his fanatical persistence, kings, popes, ecclesiastics, legists and statesmen found themselves forced to express their views on the matter, which became known as the 'Great Cause'. In his dealings with Scotland, Edward's bad qualities came to the surface: his lack of imagination, insensitivity, intransigence, intolerance and brutality. We may go as far as to say that his short-sighted policy towards Scotland disqualifies him to some extent from being regarded as a great king. What great king would imperil the safety and prosperity of his country by insisting on the public humiliation of a weak neighbouring kingdom, fundamentally well disposed towards his own country, at the very moment when he needed his hands free to repel the French invasion of Gascony? And this was the same Edward who, in his efforts to arbitrate between the Emperor-elect, Rudolf of Habsburg, and the princes of Savoy, and between the Angevin King of Sicily and Peter the Great of Aragon, saw himself as the inheritor of the great mediating role of St Louis.

Edward's mistaken policy towards Scotland, dating from the tragic death at sea of the little Maid of Norway in 1290, coloured the last years of his reign. All at once nothing went right for this able and energetic monarch: he was duped by his overlord Philip the Fair as he was to dupe his vassal John Balliol; the alliance of kings and princes of the Rhineland and the Low Countries, which he painstakingly formed by bribes and marriages to provide a strong eastern front in his war against the French, was weakened by the defection of Adolph of Nassau; the Welsh rose in revolt once again; the leading magnates refused to fight for their King in Gascony; Edward arbitrarily seized the nation's wool; he outlawed the clergy; he was no longer trusted by Parliament and could only get the money he needed by agreeing to reconfirm the Magna Carta and the Charter of the Forest. In France his temporising policies were ineffective and foreshadowed the Hundred Years' War; and in

OPPOSITE Part of the Scottish reply to Edward's demand for recognition of his sovereignty in June 1291. After the death of Alexander III of Scotland, since there was no obvious choice for a successor, Edward was invited to settle the dispute between rival competitors for the Crown. He insisted that they first recognised his overlordship which they eventually agreed to do.

Sire la bone gent descoce que lautre iour vieudrent a Norham par vre requeste e les
tres qil poent auoir dedenz si brief temps vous maundent saluz par nous et vous
rcient mout de la bone volunte que vous auez enuers le Royaume descoce e la bone
nt de la terre e encore auerez si vous plest car il entendent qil ne ount autre chose deshuy
deseruiront si dieu plest. Et vous maundent sire qils ount entendu la monstraunce
e feust lautre iour faite en lesglise de Norham en vre presence par le bonchef Rogier
ribazoun vre Chivaler la quele est tele sicome ils ont entendu que vous ditez qe vous
z chief seignur du Royaume descoce e qe lauantdit Royaume est tenue de vous en chief
nt vous requistez la bone gent que la furent qils vousissent aorder a vous come a chief
gnour e qe vous les meyntiendrez en pees e en quiete solonc les loys e les usages du
iaume descoce. Et pource qe vous ne entendez ne ne voulez que nul home soit desheri
si volez qe les demaundantz qui droit cleiment eu Royaume monstrent en vre presence
droit qe chescun quide auoir et vous vre droit monstrer volez e par vre conseil e le conseil
la bone gent du Roiaume resoun e droit ferrez a chescun.

cest la responce fait e done a le Roi dengletere par les dittes home descote touchant la demande de soverein seigneurie du Roialme descoce qe le dit Roi dengletere ad demande

Sire a ceste monstraunce vous respoignent la bone gent que icy nous ont enuoiez qils
entendent mie que si graunte chose demaundriez si bon droit ne entendisez auoir. Mes de
droit rien ne sieuent ne par vous ne par voz auncestres vnques demaunde e use ne ne
ent dount ils vous respoignent tant come en eaux est qe a vre monstraunce ne ount
poair a respondre saunz seignur a qui la demaunde doit estre faite e qui poair en auera
respondre car sil feust ensi qe ils se assentissent a vre demaunde rien ne acresteroit a vous
droit ne de proffit ne descresteroit a lour lige seignour mes bien volent la bone gent
Roiaume que celuy qui Roi serra en lauantdit Royaume face a vous quantqz reson e
ntre demaunde. Car il poair auera de respondre e faire e nul autre. Ne lour
ble que autre responce vous purront faire sauue le serment qils firent apres
mort le Roy e la generale sentence donee par Euesques Abbes e autres prelatz sur

Scotland he bequeathed, by his misplaced toughness, an impossible legacy to his unfortunate son Edward II.

The historian F. W. Maitland advised us to 'think the thoughts of our ancestors', difficult as such a thing can be. Why was Edward so convinced that the kings of England had, since time immemorial, been the overlords of the kings of Scotland? There had always, it seems, been at least two kingdoms in this island. Until the end of the eleventh century Scotland was an isolated and obscure country and the English had not attempted to define their relationship with the northern kingdom. Scotland emerged from the shadows with the marriage of King Malcolm III (1058–93) to Margaret, a great-niece of Edward the Confessor, in about 1070. This is the Malcolm in Shakespeare's *Macbeth*.

In the twelfth century, Anglo-Normans penetrated into the lowlands. Scottish baronial families, like the Bruces and Balliols, held lands on both sides of the border; the two royal families were becoming increasingly intermarried; Scottish power moved southwards and controlled Northumberland, Cumberland and Westmorland, as well the enormous earldom of Huntingdon. The Scottish Church had, like the monarchy, moved out of its period of Celtic isolation and had become a province of the western Church. It was necessary to decide where its allegiance lay: as it had no archbishop of its own, it tended either to acknowledge the supremacy of the metropolitan see of York or the direct authority of the papacy. During the thirteenth century the Scottish Church was a *filia specialis* (special daughter) of the Holy See.

The main theme in the history of the relations between England and Scotland in the Middle Ages was the recurrent claim of the English king that the king of Scotland held his realm as a vassal of the king of England. As the atmosphere of the Middle Ages became more scholastic and legalistic, so a vast literature gathered around this question, with the arguments on both sides becoming more and more far-flung and fanciful. In Edward's letter to Boniface VIII in 1301 he traced the feudal ties binding Scotland to England back to the time of the Trojan

War. In fact, all these supposed inherent rights were imaginary: there had never been a fundamental treaty between England and Scotland, like that between Henry and St Louis in 1259, which could be used as a starting-point for questions of vassalage and other matters. The problem was not one on which the legists brooded incessantly; it generally cropped up at the beginning of a new reign in Scotland when there was some particularly difficult situation. In Edward's reign there were two such times: the 'interregnum' after the death of the Maid of Norway and the period after the deposition of Balliol as King of Scotland.

Seal of Alexander III, King of Scotland from 1249 to 1286, who was married to Henry III's daughter. Peace between England and Scotland continued unbroken during Alexander's reign.

The first treaty that we know of which touches on the question is one of 1174 between Henry II and William the Lion. In it the English demand for the homage of Scotland was uncompromisingly stated. William submitted, but later he claimed that he had been acting under coercion as a prisoner. In 1189 Richard I absolved him from his allegiance, but whether this meant that William and his heirs were released for all time from allegiance for the realm of Scotland was never clear. William thought that the treaty applied to the direct homage of certain Scottish magnates to the English Crown and he continued to behave as if he accepted English suzerainty. Be that as it may, the question was never far beneath the surface in Anglo-Scottish relations, and Edward was to see to it that, in the name of the 'Great Cause', they were to be cruelly bedevilled for centuries to come.

It was the Scottish Church, rather than the Crown, which seemed the most anxious for independence. It welcomed becoming a *filia specialis* of Rome and the Holy See, at times at any rate, though it encouraged the Scottish Kings Alexander II (1214–49) and Alexander III (1249–86) to recognise the overlordship of the English King in the reign of the family-minded Henry III. Henry's sister Joan married Alexander II and his daughter Margaret married Alexander III. In 1238, when Joan died childless, a crisis of succession threatened. The story went about that Alexander declared young Robert Bruce, his great-nephew, to be his heir. Then the Scottish King married

Marie de Coucy, of an important French family, who in 1241 bore him a son and heir, Henry's future son-in-law.

Scots in the fourteenth and fifteenth centuries looked back upon the reigns of the two Alexanders as a golden age, although Margaret who, at the age of eleven, was whisked away from home at Windsor to become Queen of Scotland, found it a horrible place. She was kept in solitary confinement in Edinburgh Castle and was looked upon with suspicion as a representative of English influence. She acquired greater liberty of action after her husband attained his majority. During the years of Alexander III's minority, Henry showed much solicitude about the welfare of the young couple and he exercised a benevolent supervision over Scottish affairs. Edward was to exercise a similar supervision after the death of Alexander III in 1286 when various claimants came forward for the Scottish Crown.

Relations between Henry and his brother-in-law, Alexander II, had not been all that good, in spite of the family ties between the two royal houses. The Scottish King had not only sided with the rebels during the English civil war of 1216–17, but had also later chosen to revive the old claim of the Scottish kings to Northumberland, Cumberland and Westmorland. A treaty was concluded in York with the help of the papal legate, Cardinal Otto, whereby Alexander abandoned his claim to these northern counties, obtaining some English lands in compensation. Under the terms of the treaty Alexander was given £200 worth of land in Northumberland and Cumberland, 'if two hundred pounds' worth could be found in those counties outside towns where there are castles'. It was further stated in the treaty that the King of the Scots and his heirs enjoyed in this territory:

> Every liberty and free custom and immunity, in woodland and open land, in meadows and pastures, in waters and mills, in roads and paths, in ponds and fish-pools, in marshes and fisheries, with soc and sac, tol and team, infangenthef and utfangenfeth, hamsoken, grithbreche, bloodwite, fihtwite, ferdwite, hengwite, leyrwite, flymenafyrmth, murder, theft and forestall, in season and

out of season, and in all places. The King of Scots, and his heirs, and all his men in those lands, shall be free and quite from every scot and geld, and from aids of sheriffs and of all their servants, and from hidage, carucagen, danegeld, horngeld, military services, wapentakes, scutages, tallages, lastages, stallages, shires, hundreds, guards, wardpenny, averpenny, hundredpenny, burghalpenny, tithingpenny, and from maintenance of castles, parks, bridges and closes, and from carriage, summage and navage, and from the building of royal houses, and every kind of workservice.

The delightful wording of the treaty, originally written in Latin, is one reason for reproducing part of it here; another is to show the delicate jurisdictional state of affairs which existed between the two neighbouring kingdoms and the remarkable influence exerted by Cardinal Otto. Scotland was relatively free of the conflict between lay and ecclesiastical jurisdiction, which was so marked a feature of the reign of Edward I. The Church in Scotland was determined to maintain its direct dependence

The Free Warren Charter, a grant for game rights in the demesne lands of Roger de Pilkington and his heirs in the county of Lancaster, awarded in 1291 by Edward at Norham where he was adjudicating on the claims to the Scottish throne. The animals depicted on the charter are those which Pilkington was allowed to shoot.

upon the Holy See, and the popes, by refusing to appoint an archbishop, found themselves responsible for a large part of the administration of the country. They chose their bishops and judges with great care. The use of judges delegate, generally Scotsmen, has been regarded as the most remarkable legal feature of thirteenth-century Scotland. A practical arrangement was worked out between the lay and ecclesiastical systems. Bishops and abbots worked together with earls and magnates as the guardians of social order and as advisers to the king. The pious and clerically-minded Henry would have welcomed such an arrangement in England, and in fact it did to a certain extent obtain there at various periods of his reign. Henry must have felt satisfied with the general state of affairs in Scotland, and he must have enjoyed the easy-going, family relationship which existed between the two Courts, one which was much the same as that existing between the French and English Courts. He certainly felt himself responsible, in a rather vague way, for the fortunes of his son-in-law and daughter.

Henry's protection was particularly necessary for the young Alexander until he attained his majority. His minority lasted for thirteen years, from 1249 to 1262. In 1255 Henry came north to rescue his son-in-law from certain 'rebel' councillors; he established a new Scottish council of government, consisting of famous names such as the Earls of Fife, Dunbar, Strathearn and Carrick who were to hold office until Alexander came of age. They displaced other councillors who had made life unpleasant for the young couple; those removed included the Comyns, Earls of Menteith and Buchan, John Balliol and Robert de Ros. Henry could not bear to think of his daughter being unhappy or maltreated, so the young King and his councillors had to swear that 'we will treat and guard his daughter, our queen, in matrimonial affection, with every sort of consideration which befits our queen and the daughter of so great a Prince, and we shall cause due and proper honours to be shown to her, in our realm, in every possible way.' This arrangement was soon followed by another *coup d'état*, when Alexander was seized by the Comyns at Kinross. Henry approved the composition of the new council which included the Bishop of St Andrews, Alexander Comyn, Earl of Buchan, the Earl of Mar and the Queen Mother, now married to John of Acre, son of the King of Jerusalem. After Alexander came of age in 1262, the long peace between Scotland and England continued unbroken until his death in 1286.

The border between the two countries was never systematically fortified so that barons like the Balliols and Bruces, with

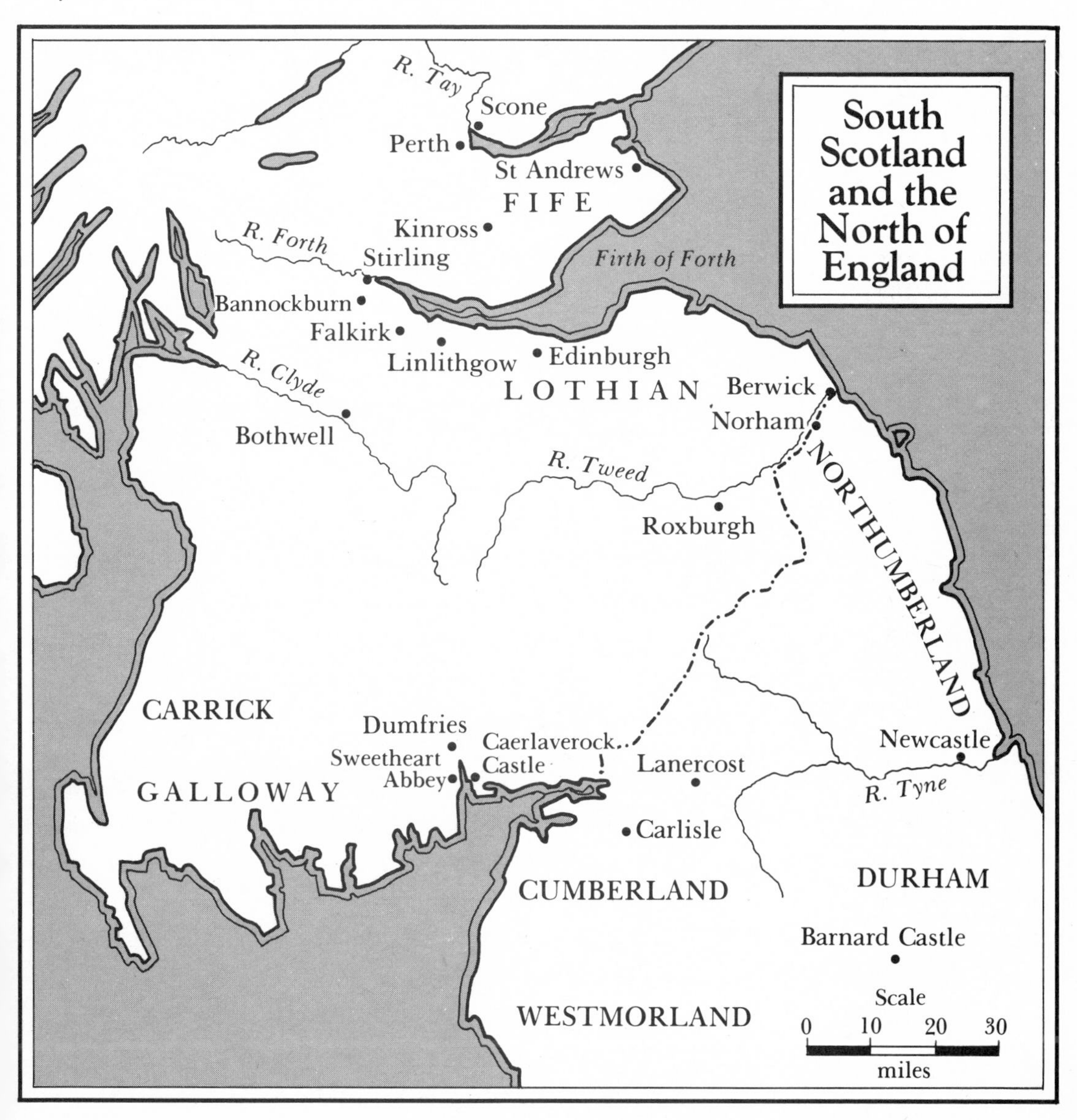

lands in both kingdoms, had few problems of divided loyalties although serving two kings. No formal, thorough delineation of the border was undertaken, and the occasional dispute was generally settled by a 'perambulation' of knights jointly chosen by both sides. The Scottish nobles who had large estates and were influential at Court were largely of Norman descent, although there were some of Breton and Flemish origin. By marrying into ancient Scottish families, and acquiring properties and earldoms in Scotland, these high-ranking magnates came to believe that they had as good a right to the throne as any of their fellows when the succession was no longer clear. With their cosmopolitan backgrounds, they provided a

The Royal House of Scotland

showing the claims of Balliol and Bruce

- DAVID I (r. 1124-53)
  - Henry
    - MALCOLM IV (r. 1153-65)
      - HENRY III, King of England (r. 1216-72)
        - EDWARD I, King of England (r. 1272-1307)
          - EDWARD II, King of England (r. 1307-27)
        - Margaret m. ALEXANDER III (r. 1249-86) (1); m. (2) Yolande
          - Margaret m. Erik II of Norway
            - Margaret, the Maid of Norway (d. 1290)
    - WILLIAM THE LYON (r. 1165-1214)
      - ALEXANDER II (r. 1214-49)
        - ALEXANDER III (r. 1249-86) m. (1) Margaret, m. (2) Yolande
    - David, Earl of Huntingdon (d. 1219) m. Maud, d. of Hugh of Chester
      - Margaret m. Lord of Galloway
        - Dervorguilla m. John Balliol
          - JOHN BALLIOL (r. 1292-6, d. 1313)
      - Isabella m. Robert Bruce Lord of Annandale
        - Robert Bruce (d. 1295)
          - Robert Bruce (d. 1304)
            - ROBERT I (r. 1306-29)
              - Margery m. Walter, the Steward
                - Stuart Kings
              - DAVID II (r. 1329-71)
            - Edward
            - Nigel

pro-English element in Scottish society, as long as their Scottish susceptibilities were not outraged – which in due course they were by Edward. Among the leading figures were the Balliols of Galloway and of Barnard Castle in Durham, the Bruces (or Brus) of Carrick, Annandale and Yorkshire, and the Comyns of Badenoch. The Comyns were descended from a clerk who had come north from England in the middle of the twelfth century. It is well, then, to remember that many of the most influential Scottish families were, up to the end of the thirteenth century, well disposed towards England and welcomed the softening influence of English culture in their harsh but appealing country.

The great tragedy of British history in the thirteenth century was the premature death of Alexander III, at the age of forty-four, in a riding accident in 1286, and of his grand-daughter, the Maid of Norway, in 1290. Immediately after Alexander's death, Edward set out for Gascony where he stayed for three years. The regents, acting on behalf of the Maid of Norway, managed to govern Scotland without much difficulty. After Edward's return in 1289 elaborate arrangements were made for a marriage between the Maid and his only surviving son, Edward of Caernarvon, aged six and five respectively, which would have brought about the union of the two kingdoms. The death of the Maid in the Orkneys on her way from Norway to Scotland shattered these hopes. But Edward at this moment had thoughts only for his own wife, Eleanor, who was dying at Harby near Lincoln.

'The child of so many hopes'

The deaths of the two Queens in 1290 soured and hardened Edward, now aged fifty-one. A few weeks earlier he had been at the top of his form, just back from Gascony, having settled once and for all, so he thought, territorial arguments with France. He had recently married his daughter Joan of Acre to the Earl of Gloucester, one of his most important and troublesome subjects, while his son was betrothed to the Maid of Norway, 'the child of so many hopes'. Another daughter, Margaret, had married John, heir to the dukedom of Brabant, as part of Edward's policy of containing the ambitions of Philip the Fair. As a crowning act to a successful reign, he announced that he would go on a Crusade. (Acre, the last Christian stronghold in the Holy Land, fell the following year). Then, suddenly, these two calamities took place. After giving touching expression of his love for his deceased wife, whom he later commemorated by erecting the Eleanor Crosses, Edward turned his attention not to his Crusade, but to Scotland.

Two drawings from the Seton Armorial of 1591, showing the two contenders for the Scottish throne with their coats of arms embroidered on their wives' dresses.
RIGHT John Balliol who reigned from 1292 to 1296.
OPPOSITE Robert Bruce whose reign began in 1306.

The Scottish magnates were displaying unseemly disunity in the choice of an heir to the Maid. In their perplexity and mutual animosity they all, earls, magnates and claimants alike, turned to Edward for advice and protection. Most of them had rallied to the cause of Robert Bruce, but the powerful Bishop of St Andrews and John Comyn of Badenoch aggressively pushed forward the claims of John Balliol. All the candidates, including

Bruce and Balliol, were comparatively remote from the royal line; these Anglo-Normans had difficulty in producing genealogies which revealed pure Scottish descent and when they did so, their claims were often tarnished by marriages with illegitimate offspring of the sovereign. Edward was in a genuine predicament: the Scottish magnates, many of whom owed him allegiance for their English lands, had invited him to determine a dispute for the solution of which there was no formal machinery. It was essential for him to be accorded some sort of status which, short of naked force, would make his verdict authoritative. This was what he now set about to obtain.

In the parish church of Norham, near the Bishop of Durham's castle, seven miles from Berwick, the debate on the Great Cause opened in 1291 with a statement by Roger Brabagon, one of Edward's judges who was later to announce the award:

> Our Lord the King has observed the peace of the realm of Scotland to be disturbed by the deaths of King Alexander and of his children, who were kinsfolk of our Lord the King (by which deaths he is greatly distressed) and in his desire to do right to all those who can make any claim to the inheritance of the Kingdom of Scotland, and in order to keep the peace among the people, he has asked you, the good people of the realm, to come here, because of a certain matter which he wished to explain to you. He himself has come hither from a distant place, in order that by virtue of the overlordship which belongs to him he may do justice to everyone, and, after all disturbances have been quelled, may restore settled peace to the Kingdom of Scotland. He does not propose to take anything from anybody without just cause, nor to delay any man's receiving of his right, nor to disturb nor diminish his franchise, but only to do justice to everyone as sovereign. And in order that this matter may be brought to a satisfactory conclusion, our Lord the King asks for your kind agreement, and for recognition of his overlordship, and he wishes to act with your advice in doing and executing justice.

Throughout the summer months of 1291 the competitors for the Scottish Crown and their lawyers discussed and argued with

Edward and his lawyers his claim to be the superior or direct lord of Scotland, which would include the right to sit as the judge of a court with authority to enforce its decisions in Scotland. His clerks had been busy digging into ancient chronicles and claimed to have found all sorts of fantastic material to elucidate the past relationship between the two crowns. In the end the Scottish nobles accepted the findings of the 'comprehensive historical survey'; each competitor swore publicly to accept Edward as lord of Scotland and that to him alone belonged the 'sovereign lordship of Scotland and the right to determine our several pretensions'. He was recognised as the sovereign lord while the Scottish throne was vacant, and the realm was resigned into his hands.

The hearings only came to an official end in November 1292. There were thirteen competitors, six of whom were illegitimate descendants of William the Lyon and Alexander II. Only one competitor was related to the royal house by paternal descent. The three most convincing claimants – Balliol, Bruce and John

The ruins of Norham Castle which belonged to the Bishop of Durham during Edward's reign. At the parish church of Norham, hard by the castle, the debate on the Great Cause took place in 1291.

The coronation of John Balliol, from a manuscript dating from *c.* 1310.

OPPOSITE Sweetheart Abbey in Galloway, south of Dumfries, where Archbishop Winchelsey delivered the papal order from Boniface VIII to Edward, commanding him to refrain from hostilities in Scotland, a country which belonged to the Holy See. The Abbey was founded by Dervorguilla, the mother of John Balliol, to enshrine her husband's heart.

Hastings of Abergavenny – were descended from daughters of William the Lyon's brother, David, Earl of Huntingdon. Bruce, now over eighty (the grandfather of the great Robert Bruce, of spider fame, who crushed the English at Bannockburn), was a generation older than his two cousins; although he stood a degree nearer the common ancestor, he was the son of the second daughter of David, whereas Balliol was the grandson of the eldest. For this reason, Edward and his 105 counsellors or assessors decided that Balliol had the strongest claim, and so, on 17 November 1292, Edward gave the kingdom, whole and undivided, to John Balliol who swore loyalty to his suzerain. Before the end of the month he was crowned at Scone.

John Balliol turned out to be a weak and indifferent sovereign. He did not have the strength of character of Robert Bruce and his young grandson, the future king, now aged eighteen. Balliol was not well known in Scotland, and only owed his vast estates in Northumberland, Durham and Galloway to the deaths of his brother and his mother Dervorguilla. Edward, after his exemplary and impartial adjudication at Norham, now made the fatal mistake of humiliating Balliol. Weak as he was, he reacted strongly as soon as Edward made it clear that he now regarded Balliol as an ordinary feudal vassal and that the right to hear appeals from Scottish courts in England belonged to him as sovereign lord. Edward maintained that the assembly at Norham had decided that Scotland, although impartible (i.e. indivisible), was not independent. He claimed that he had every right to summon Balliol to Westminster, just as Philip the Fair summoned Edward to Paris as Duke of Aquitaine. He should have let his own claims recede into the background, and tried to retain Scottish goodwill by continuing to pursue a policy of enlightened and disinterested good neighbourliness. He should have known, as Duke of Aquitaine, how Balliol's indignant subjects would react to his insistence upon hearing appeals against Balliol's judgments in Scotland.

The crisis came in 1295 when Balliol was summoned to Westminster to answer an appeal from Macduff of Fife against a

judgment of imprisonment imposed upon him by the Scottish Parliament meeting at Scone. Balliol went to Westminster, 'a lamb among wolves', and refused to answer Macduff's appeal. 'The King of Scotland', a Parliamentary report records, 'says that he dare not and cannot answer here on any matter touching his realm without consulting the people of his realm.' However, simply by going to Westminster, Balliol had forfeited his authority with the Scottish magnates, who now took things into their own hands. With Edward still engaged in war in Gascony, it seemed the right occasion to make a treaty with his enemy, Philip the Fair. The 'Auld Alliance' was hurriedly made between France and Scotland, a treaty which was to affect Scottish cultural and political history for the next three centuries. It included provision for a marriage between Balliol's son, Edward, and Jeanne of Valois, niece of Philip the Fair.

War between England and Scotland was now inevitable. However, before a vassal could make war on his lord, he had to sever the feudal bond in a formal *diffidatio* or renunciation of homage and fealty. On 9 April 1296, at Berwick Castle, Edward was given Balliol's formal *diffidatio*. In it Balliol spoke of the 'naked force, grievous and intolerable injuries, slights and wrongs upon us . . . for instance by summoning us outside our realm at the mere beck and call of anybody, as your own whim dictated, and by harassing us unjustifiably . . . and so by the present letter we renounce the fealty and homage which we have done to you'.

Edward's vengeance was swift. He summoned Balliol to meet him at Berwick. His nobles refused to let him go and Edward stormed and sacked the city; over 7,000 inhabitants were put to the sword and within a few days one of Europe's most active centres of commerce had sunk to being a minor seaport. Balliol submitted, surrendered his realm and left Scotland never to return. For a time he lived in Hertford with his son Edward; when in 1297 William Wallace rose in Balliol's name, father and son were transferred to the Tower of London. A couple of years later they moved to Normandy and Balliol died in 1315, the year after the Battle of Bannockburn. He left

Scotland with a bad grace, declaring that he had met nothing there but 'malice, deceit, treason and treachery' and that it was not his intention 'to enter or go into the realm of Scotland at any time to come'.

After Edward accepted the submission of the Scottish magnates at Berwick in 1296 the land appeared to lie at his feet. All the lowland castles were under his control; some of them, like Berwick, Stirling, Bothwell and Linlithgow, were of great strategic importance, controlling valley roads or key river-crossings. North of the Firth of Forth Edward personally accepted the surrender of many more castles from Auchterader to Elgin, and from St Andrews to Aberdeen. What should he now have done to create in Scotland a situation which would satisfy the national pride of nobility and people and their

The siege of Berwick from a fourteenth-century manuscript. After Balliol had renounced his feudal bond with Edward, Edward quickly took vengeance. Having stormed and sacked the city of Berwick as an example of his power, he forced Balliol into submission.

OPPOSITE John Balliol, King of the Scots, does homage to Edward I as his overlord. By this act of abasement Balliol alienated his fellow Scottish nobles who gave their support to Robert Bruce instead.

acceptance of his benevolent overlordship? Perhaps he should have offered the Crown to Robert Bruce, son of the octogenarian claimant who had died in 1295. He apparently wanted it, and Edward is reported to have said to him, 'Have I nought else to do, but to win a kingdom for you?' What he did was obviously mistaken. He had the Stone of Destiny (Stone of Scone), on which Scottish sovereigns were wont to be crowned, removed to London; he appointed at Berwick a triumvirate of Englishmen to run the country – Earl Warenne (Guardian of the land); Sir Hugh de Cressingham (Treasurer) and Sir Walter of Amersham (Chancellor). After a few days he left Scotland, not noticing the clouds gathering in the south-west, whence that outlaw knight William Wallace, the Scottish Joan of Arc, would start his meteoric rise, almost unexampled in history.

On the subject of Scottish castles, it is a curious thing that Edward I never built any castles in Scotland such as those in Wales which had 'insured' his conquests so successfully against the 'fire of rebellion'. In Wales he had built in stone on sites carefully chosen for their strategic value; in Scotland he simply

Linlithgow Castle in Lothian, one of the lowland castles which were of great strategic importance to Edward after his success at Berwick.

e frederic occupa lezille apres lui. Commen

e roy descoce fu amenez au roy dengleterre e

William Wallace, one of the greatest fighters for the freedom of Scotland. He recovered much of the lost lands of Scotland in the year of 1297, but his success was short-lived: in 1298 Edward returned to win a great victory at Falkirk, forcing Wallace into hiding and eventually to his execution.

built in timber in places where there was already a tower and moat. And yet he had retained the services of all those masons and carpenters who had planned the Welsh castles, and they accompanied his armies into Scotland. Even in Berwick, designed to be the administrative base of his Scottish campaign, he merely tinkered with an existing castle, badly situated in relation to the town. Had Edward built strong castles, he might have imposed his overlordship on Scotland as successfully as he had on Wales. Why did he not do so? Perhaps it was because he never gave his undivided attention to Scotland, always thinking that each campaign would be the last; he must also have realised that his Exchequer would not have been able to supply the funds for another ambitious castle-building programme. All he did was to take possession of the existing castles, 'to strengthen them with ditch and peel and brattice, and to hope that his enemies would acknowledge themselves to be beaten'.

The following year, in the spring of 1297, Wallace appeared on the scene, and by the autumn he had recovered all Scotland except Roxburgh and Berwick. He fought in the name of John Balliol, who was perhaps at that very moment making those derogatory remarks about his country. Wallace's success was short-lived: Edward returned in wrath, and in 1298 there took place the great English victory at Falkirk. Wallace escaped and was not captured until 1305, when he was executed in London in the usual gory way. The monks of Lanercost Priory, where Edward was later, during his last Scottish campaign in 1306–7, to lie ill for five months, tell us that Wallace was captured by 'a certain Scot, to wit, Sir John de Menteith, and was taken to London to the king, and it was adjudged that he should be drawn and hanged, beheaded, disembowled, and dismembered, and that his entrails should be burnt; which was done. And his head was exposed upon London Bridge, his right arm on the bridge of Newcastle-upon-Tyne, his left at Aberdeen.' Wallace would certainly have treated his opponents with equal brutality: his sword-belt was covered with the skin, cut into strips, of an English tax-collector who had fallen at the Battle of Stirling Bridge, where Wallace defeated Warenne, Earl of Surrey.

In 1299, the year after the victory of Falkirk, Pope Boniface VIII ordered Edward to stop hostilities in a land which belonged to the Holy See. Archbishop Winchelsey delivered, rather reluctantly, this papal order to Edward at Sweetheart Abbey in Galloway, south of Dumfries. Edward did not take Boniface's exhortation very well. The Jubilee of 1300 was about to reveal the Pope in the full glamour of his power and his famous bull, *Unam Sanctam*, of 1302 was to define, once and for all, the extreme claims of papal authority. Later Boniface, under

increasing pressure from Philip the Fair, revealed a complete change of mind and confirmed that Edward was overlord of Scotland.

It looked once again as if Scotland would accept a permanent peace under Edward's remote control. Edward placed Scotland under the rule of three regents: Bishop Lamberton of St Andrews, John Comyn (known as the Red Baron) and Robert Bruce. The campaign of 1297–8 was followed by others in 1298, 1299–1300, 1300, 1301 and 1303–4. Edward had a firm grip of the country south of the Forth and a very loose one further north. It seemed as if it would be impossible to dislodge him from Scotland. Then Robert Bruce unexpectedly rebelled in 1306. He murdered John Comyn at Dumfries and was crowned King of Scotland at Scone a few weeks later. Edward learned the news at Winchester in February. He lost no time in mobilising an army. As his health was failing he had to be carried northwards in a litter, reaching Lanercost Priory in October 1306. Bruce returned to the attack after several months in hiding. Although sick, Edward was determined to take the field himself. 'But alas!' in the words of the faithful Lanercost Chronicle, 'On the feast of the translation of St Thomas, Archbishop of Canterbury and Martyr, this illustrious and excellent king, my Lord Edward, son of King Henry, died at Burgh-upon-Sands, which is distant about three miles to the north of Carlisle . . . throughout his time he had been fearless and warlike, in all things strenuous and illustrious; he left not his like among Christian princes for sagacity and courage.' The day was 7 July 1307 and Edward was in his sixty-eighth year.

The two great enterprises which had occupied Edward's thoughts towards the end of his life were the subjection of Scotland and the recovery of the Holy Land. He hoped to share in those great works even after his death. He begged his son to carry his bones about with him in the Scottish campaigns so that even when dead he might still lead his warriors to victory against the hated enemy. He also requested that his heart be sent to the Holy Land with a train of a hundred knights to fight for the recovery of the Holy Selpulchre. Edward II set these dying

OPPOSITE The coronation chair made for Edward I to enclose the Stone of Scone, which he seized from the Scots in 1297. Made of oak, the chair was painted with birds, foliage and animals on a gilt background, and faint traces of these remain. Since 1308 every sovereign of England, except Edward V and Edward VIII, has been crowned on this chair.

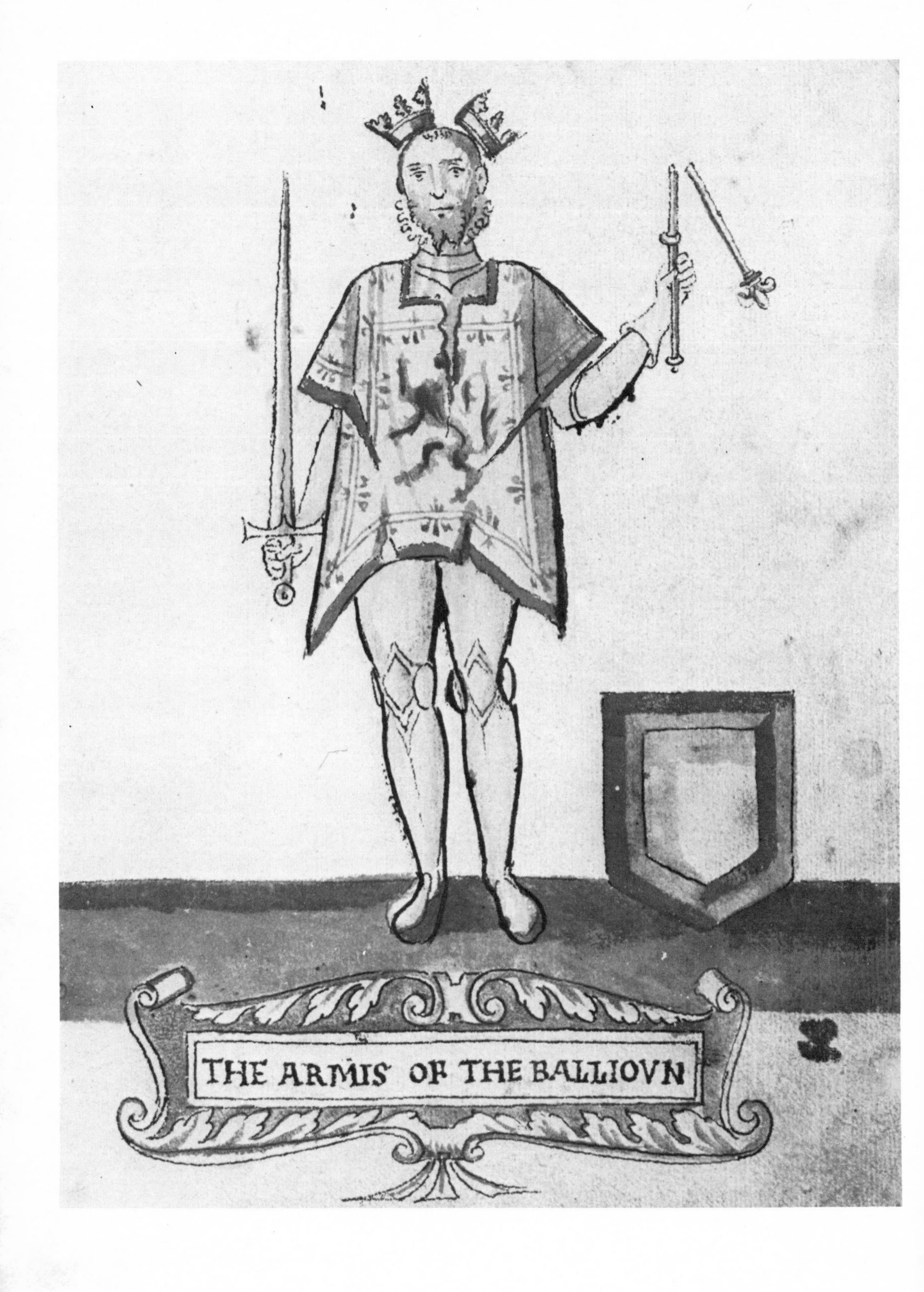
THE ARMIS OF THE BALLIOVN

wishes at nought: his father's body was unceremoniously bundled off to Westminster Abbey for immediate burial; and the campaign in Scotland was abandoned at once. Edward II proved quite incapable of consolidating his father's gains in Scotland. While he was busy in England indulging his favourites, Robert Bruce started to reconquer his lands. Not until 1314 did Edward II turn his attention to Scotland, and in June of that year an English army of 20,000 suffered the most devastating defeat at the Battle of Bannockburn – a defeat which brought to an end all English claims to overlordship of Scotland.

OPPOSITE The downfall of John Balliol: a broken sceptre and crown.

Although it now appears obvious that Edward I was wrong regarding Scotland and that he had little chance of subduing permanently that stubborn race, we should perhaps temper the severity of our judgment of his Scottish policy by looking at the Great Cause through contemporary eyes. It was the belief of medieval rulers, whether of Church or State, that the defence of their inherited rights was their highest and most sacred duty. The zest for defending legal claims, although going to absurd lengths – as in the case of Edward invoking Trojan history to support his claim to overlordship of Scotland – did a great deal to mould Western civilisation and society. Some of his advocates have tended to idealise him and see in him an impartial arbitrator like St Louis at the Mise of Amiens in 1264. Edward was no St Louis, but more of the stamp of Philip the Fair and Charles of Anjou. He had himself experienced the ineffectiveness of arbitration when not backed by force. Edward may also have thought that simple arbitration would have implied the abandonment of his claim to homage. He would certainly have believed that his coronation oath forbade him in any way to diminish the rights of his Crown. In any event, it is clear that he needed little persuading either from custom, contemporaries or tradition to pursue the role of the 'Hammer of the Scots'.

8 Husband and Fathe

74-1307

PREVIOUS PAGES The heads of Edward I and Queen Margaret carved on the canopy above the tomb of Gervase Alard, appointed by Edward to the office of Admiral of the Fleet, in Winchelsea Church. Edward married Margaret, the sister of Philip IV, in 1299.

EDWARD WAS LUCKY in the wife that his father chose for him. The arranged marriage at the Monastery of Las Huelgas in 1254, when Edward was fifteen and Eleanor nine, turned out to be one of history's love matches. Eleanor of Castile was a dark-haired Spanish beauty; the guiding principle of her life was, as far as one can judge, providing for her husband's comfort and subjecting herself to his will. She led the life of an exalted camp follower, bearing him children wherever he happened to be campaigning – in the Holy Land, Gascony and Wales.

Eleanor is perhaps the best loved of all English queen-consorts, but she was not nearly as popular in her own lifetime as she later became. In fact, at the time there was little to chose between the public disapproval of her and her mother-in-law, Eleanor of Provence. The elder Eleanor had her hated Savoyard uncles to fan the xenophobia of the Londoners, while the younger surrounded herself with her flashy, extravagant Spanish relations. She brought with her from Spain many tapestries to decorate her rooms in Westminster Palace and the Savoy Palace in the Strand. She had a reputation for being grasping, as well as pious and virtuous. She overtaxed her tenants and joined forces with Jewish usurers to gain possession of estates belonging to Christians. Nobody who looks at her delicate effigy in Westminster Abbey would have thought her capable of doing such things.

Eleanor does not seem to have bothered much about the thirteen children – four sons and nine daughters – which she bore to Edward. Neither she nor her husband created for them the happy atmosphere which characterised the family life of Henry and Eleanor of Provence. The elder Eleanor, unlike her daughter-in-law, was affectionate and solicitous about the welfare of her grandchildren. She worried about how their parents' long absences abroad would affect them. At least two of the children died when Edward and Eleanor were in the Holy Land and elsewhere from 1270 to 1274. When Edward of Caernarvon was two, his parents went to Gascony for three years (1286–9), and his mother died within fifteen months of her

Eleanor of Castile, Edward I's first wife, from a sculpture in Lincoln Cathedral.

return to England. The children must have been a rather sickly brood, for of the thirteen few survived their parents and only one, Mary, the Nun of Amesbury, reached the age of fifty.

The Queen died at Harby in Nottinghamshire on 28 November 1290. Great was the King's grief. Her corpse was taken to Lincoln where the entrails and heart were removed for separate burial, the former in the Cathedral, the latter in the

Dominican church in London where the heart of her son, Alfonso, had been placed six years before. The embalmed body was ceremoniously conveyed from Lincoln to Westminster in twelve stages, accompanied for most of the way by the King and his Court. The inconsolable Edward ordered a monumental display to commemorate his wife, more elaborate than was ever accorded to any English king or queen before or since. At each of the twelve places where the bier rested for the night a memorial cross was erected: at Lincoln, Grantham, Stamford, the royal hunting lodge at Geddington, Northampton, Stony Stratford, Woburn, Dunstable, St Albans, Waltham, West Cheap in the City of London, and King's Mews at Charing. When the bier came near its resting-place each evening, 'the King's Chancellor and the great men there present had marked a fitting place where they might afterwards erect, at the King's expense, a cross of wonderful size'.

Of the twelve Eleanor Crosses only three survive today: those at Waltham, Northampton and Geddington. The basic shape of the Waltham Cross is polygonal; the pedestals are decorated with the shields of Ponthieu, Castile, Laon and England, while above there are gabled niches with ogival arches enshrining statues of the Queen. At Geddington the pattern is triangular, producing a slender and gracious shaft adorned with statues. The Eleanor Crosses have their place in the history, not only of monumental sculpture, but of Gothic art itself: they are a manifestation of the new Decorated style, of which Edward's masons were pioneers. The idea of these commemorative crosses was probably taken from France; similar memorials had been set up twenty years earlier to mark the funeral procession which carried the bones of St Louis from Paris to St Denis.

The Queen was now dead and the six-year-old Edward was left with one parent. Although his luck was about to turn, Edward I's reputation as a warrior and a statesman was now at its height. The elaborate memorials of stone, bronze and marble which he erected for his wife inside Westminster Abbey and without were not simply signs of his devotion to her memory: they were also evidence of his desire to enhance the prestige of

OPPOSITE A watercolour of the Eleanor Cross at Waltham, Herts, by Thomas Malton Sr (*c.* 1780–90).

the monarchy by creating visible symbols of its piety and power. Edward of Caernarvon, the only surviving son (his elder brother Alfonso had died in 1284), was to be groomed for this great inheritance.

Edward's birth in Caernarvon Castle was not the great event that later legend claimed it to be. Edward I, as all schoolchildren know, had promised to find for his Welsh subjects a prince that was 'born in Wales and could speak never a word of English'. In an effort to fulfill this unlikely promise he is supposed to have presented the newborn, all-Welsh babe to his subjects from the ramparts of Caernarvon Castle. In fact Edward did not receive the principality of Wales from his father until 1301, seventeen years later. His birth in Wales was purely fortuitous, just one of Eleanor's many 'campaigning' deliveries.

What were the influences at work upon the young Edward, other than those of his father, who was to become harsher and more unsympathetic when he could no longer find money to pursue his mistaken policies? We have the paradox of Edward I exhausting himself administering his own country and fighting others, later heaping honours, titles and lands on the son who was to carry on his work, and yet taking little interest in the boy in whom he reposed his hopes.

Much sadder for Edward than the loss of his mother was that of his grandmother in 1291 at the convent of Amesbury. She disapproved of the little Edward and his household having to follow the King and his Court to the north. 'We feel uneasy about his going. When we were there, we could not avoid being ill, on account of the bad climate. We pray you therefore, deign to provide some place in the south where he can have a good and temperate climate, and dwell there while you visit the north.' One of the most striking things about the young Edward's life as a boy was the kaleidoscopic nature of his movements. It was only during the winter months that he spent more than a few days at the same place. His household was in constant motion from early April until October, visiting royal manors and monasteries. The only place where he spent more than a few months on end was the Hertfordshire manor of

OPPOSITE The Geddington Cross in Northamptonshire: one of the twelve crosses, of which only three survive today, which marked Eleanor's funeral procession from Lincoln to Westminster.

NWA WHITE

Langley, later called King's Langley, near St Albans. There he could ride (on a camel if he wished), observe and perhaps participate in the rustic arts of digging, ditching and thatching.

Before Edward was thirteen he had lost the companionship of his sisters Eleanor, Joan, Margaret and Elizabeth who had been married to Henry, Count of Bar, Gilbert of Clare, Earl of Gloucester, John, son of the Duke of Brabant, and John I, Count of Holland and Zeeland. Edward I was using his daughters as pawns in his policy of making the Low Countries a buffer against the predatory designs of Philip the Fair. Elizabeth had the strongest personality of the sisters and was never afraid of arguing with her father. It was unfortunate for her brother that he lost her spirited support in future encounters with his father.

'Had he devoted as much toil to arms as he gave to the rustic arts, England would have prospered and his name rung through the whole earth.' The chroniclers of the time and later historians had two things in particular against Edward II: that his pursuits were not aristocratic and that he was not interested in the business of government. He may have been, as psychologists might suggest, reacting against his father's enthusiastic addiction to journeying and to government. He may have been a medieval 'drop-out', believing that his father's expensive wars and interest in administration were getting the country nowhere. But during Edward II's twenty-year reign, life was probably pleasanter for the ordinary people than it had been under the 'greatest of all the Plantagenets'. The young King Edward II is pictured as being strong, handsome, weak-willed, frivolous, disliking battles, tournaments, politics and business, wishing only to please himself. His amusements were not dissipated ones, rather the opposite. He liked 'ignoble' sports such as racing, rowing, play-acting, farming, smith's work, digging and thatching – not activities normally associated with medieval gentlemen; and he pursued them, not with his fellow nobles, but with upstart courtiers and members of the lower orders. This 'depraved' side of his character came more into evidence after his father's death.

Another legend which should be dispelled is that Edward was

as a youth effeminate, indulging in various sybaritic enjoyments. We have just seen that his recreations were exceptionally manly, but it is of course possible to dig and thatch by day and be foppish at night. Historical romances tell us that when the fierce warrior-King summoned his dissipated son to his presence to remind him of his duty to continue hammering the Scots, the young Prince, lolling in a long loose cape designed for him by his friend, Gavaston, his fair hair held back by fillets of gold set with sapphires, would stifle a yawn with a slim white hand adorned with jewels. A less well-known description of him is that given by the herald-poet who wrote the Caerlaverock Roll of Arms about those who were present at the siege of the castle in the summer of 1300. Caerlaverock Castle, on the Solway Firth near Dumfries, is thought to be one of the few castles in Scotland which was fortified by Master James of St George whose genius is present in so many of the northern Welsh castles. The Caerlaverock herald-poet described the young Edward on his first Scottish campaign:

> The fourth squadron with its train,
> Edward the King's son led,
> A youth of seventeen years of age
> And newly bearing arms.
> He was of a well-proportioned and handsome person,
> Of a courteous disposition, and well bred,
> And desirous of finding an occasion
> To make proof of his strength.
> He managed his steed wonderfully well.

BELOW AND OPPOSITE
Two dancers, from a late thirteenth-century English bible.

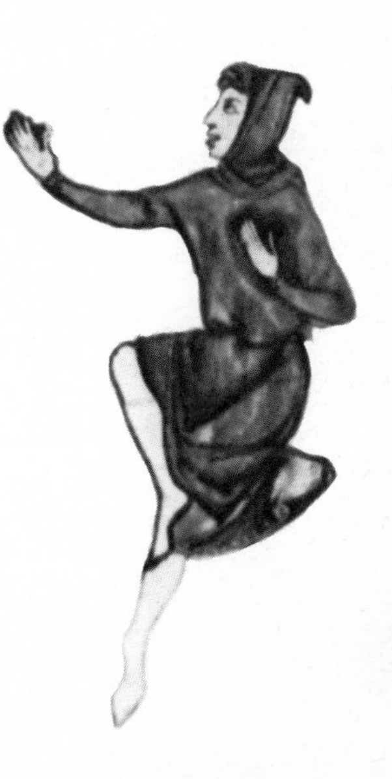

This was written in the year when Edward I's campaign in Scotland had come to a halt and he was strengthening the lowland castles after the defeat of Wallace. It was the year before Edward was solemnly invested with Wales and the palatinate of Chester.

The Caerlaverock poet's favourable description of Edward leaves us with the impression that his father must have seen that his son had a reasonably satisfactory upbringing. The basic elements of a medieval, upper-class education were a knowledge of Latin and the essentials of behaviour appropriate to a knight and gentleman in church, at Court, at tournaments and in warfare. A certain Guy Ferre was in charge of Edward's household from 1294 to 1303; he had been in the service of several members of the royal family, including Henry III, Eleanor of Provence and Edmund of Lancaster. Guy was probably responsible for turning out the young knight who appeared in the Caerlaverock poem to epitomise the values of the age, although it has been customary to infer that Edward was never proficient in Latin since he took his coronation oath in French.

Edward I used his son, like his daughters, to further his political ambitions. He twice arranged marriages for the little boy, accompanied by treaties of alliance with the countries concerned. The first was with the Maid of Norway who died at sea in 1290. The second was in 1297 with Philippa, daughter of Guy of Dampierre, Count of Flanders. This Flemish alliance

The castle of Caerlaverock fell to Edward during his Scottish campaign in 1300. The siege was commemorated by a lengthy poem which extolled the valorous part played by Edward of Caernarvon at the siege, as well as the deeds of other nobles present.

was part of Edward's north-eastern offensive against Philip the Fair who had confiscated Gascony in 1294. The alliance with the Count of Flanders was made at the beginning of 1297, and it was Edward's intention to come, at long last, to the rescue of his Gascon subjects. He had not done so earlier because he had been distracted by events at home.

With Wales permanently and Scotland temporarily subdued, Edward turned with zest to the idea of a vigorous attack on France. There had earlier been talk of a possible French invasion of England during Edward's punitive campaign in Scotland in 1296, and the citizens of London and Dover were bidden 'to obey Edward, the King's son, and the orders he perchance may give you'. There was no invasion, so the little Edward was deprived of the distinction of holding a military command at the age of eleven.

Then came the constitutional crisis of 1297 when the Earls of Hereford and Norfolk refused to take command in Gascony, Archbishop Winchelsey forbade contributions to the campaign, and the barons produced the Monstraunces, a formal statement of their grievances. Little Edward, who had hardly been aware of these dark and threatening happenings, was suddenly thrust into the political limelight when the King, in a ceremony of reconciliation with Winchelsey at Westminster, announced his departure for the campaign against Philip the Fair and asked the crowds to recognise his son as King should he not return. 'All the magnates there present did fealty to the King's son at his father's bidding, and he was acclaimed by all the people, their right hands upraised, as heir, future lord, and successor to the kingdom.' As it was, the King was only away for seven inglorious months while the thirteen-year-old boy 'ruled' with a regency council consisting of four ecclesiastics and six laymen. It is unlikely that he was aware of the import of the vital discussions going on during these months, which culminated in the King's surrender at Ghent in November 1297 to the baronial demands. The regency had averted civil war.

The King's 'second front' in Flanders came to nothing and a truce was declared with France in 1298. His experiences in

Edwardus III Rex

Flanders were to have two important consequences for his son: his friendship with Peter of Gavaston (or Piers Gaveston) and his marriage to Isabella of France. The former he came to love and the latter he came to hate. For the last seven hundred years, whenever the name of Edward II has been mentioned, it has been impossible not to think of the 'perverted' King and his *alter ego*, 'Perrot de Gaveston', as he was called in the Wardrobe accounts of Edward I's Flemish campaign.

Peter, the son of Arnold of Gavaston, a loyal Bearnese knight who fought for the King in Gascony, joined Edward I in Flanders in 1297 and found such favour with him that he was made a squire of the household. It is recorded that he was paid £4 6s. as wages from August to November in that year. The King was so taken by Gavaston that he sent him to join a group of young men of good family who were resident in his son's household. Within a short time Gavaston became their leader. 'When the King's son saw him,' says a chronicle, 'he fell so much in love that he entered upon an enduring compact with him, and chose and determined to knit an indissoluble bond of affection with him, before all other mortals'.

At about the time that Edward and Peter became friends, the plan for a Flemish marriage was abandoned. Boniface VIII annulled the nuptial contract and, in an atmosphere of improved relations between France and England, a double marriage was arranged between Edward I and Margaret, sister of Philip the Fair, and Edward of Caernarvon and Isabella, Philip's daughter. This was the young Edward's third betrothal. Unfortunately for him it proved lasting, and in 1308 he married Isabella, the 'she-wolf of France'. He came to hate her so much that 'he carried a knife in his hose to kill Queen Isabella, and had said that if he had no other weapon, he would crush her with his teeth'.

Edward I decided that the time had come for his son to play a responsible part in the campaign in Scotland. The King's prestige had been restored by the victory at Falkirk in 1298, but much remained to be done before the country could be subdued. The young Edward was put in command of the

OPPOSITE Edward II and Isabella of France from a treatise written by Walter de Milemate in 1326. Edward married Isabella, Philip IV's daughter, in 1306. Later he came to hate her, referring to her as the 'she-wolf of France'.

rearguard in the assault on Caerlaverock Castle in Galloway, where he won, as we have seen, the admiration of onlookers for his appearance and good horsemanship. The castle fell but the English were unable to follow up their victory, and the King's temper grew worse daily. The young Edward was present on the awkward occasion when Archbishop Winchelsey delivered the Pope's message ordering the King to withdraw his troops from Scotland. It was at about this time that the dangerous intimacy between the young Edward and Gavaston, who had been in Scotland on the King's staff during the summer campaign, began to ripen.

As a reward for the prowess he had shown in Scotland, Edward of Caernarvon was given the principality of Wales and Chester in 1301. This grant is a reminder of the one which the Lord Edward had received from his father almost fifty years earlier, although that was bigger still, including as it did Gascony, the Channel Islands and various English towns. Edward of Caernarvon had also inherited, on the death of his mother Eleanor, the county of Ponthieu in northern France. It fell, like Gascony, into the hands of the French in 1294. During Edward's minority the county was placed in the care of his uncle, Edmund of Lancaster, and he was still a minor when it was restored by the French in 1299. The King handed over the administration of the county to the Frescobaldi, the Florentine merchants. The revenue from all these endowments came to nearly £9,000 a year; it fell, however, far short of the young Edward's needs, especially towards the end of his father's reign when the households of both father and son were kept on a permanent war footing. Thus the young Edward, despite his large income, had very little financial independence. Furthermore Edward I controlled the appointments to his son's household, just as he did those of his wives, so his son was not free to engage whom he liked.

The years 1301–4 were good ones for father and son. The young Edward was given important commands in the Scottish campaigns, where he showed himself to be a 'chip off the old block' by the zest with which he threw himself into terrorising the Scottish countryside. 'On every side he burnt hamlets and towns, granges and granaries, empty or full.' By 1304, when he was twenty, he was recognised as the second most important person in the country, toughened by campaigning, taking part in the councils of state, and apparently in his father's confidence. This happy state of affairs came to an abrupt end one day in June 1305 at Midhurst in Sussex. The Prince had apparently spoken in insulting terms to Walter de Langton, Bishop of Chester, one of the King's most important advisers on both the domestic and international scene, a dangerous man to provoke. It was Langton, also Treasurer to the Exchequer, who had negotiated the alliances against Philip the Fair. A chronicle tells us that the King 'removed his own eldest and dearest son, Edward, Prince of Wales, from his household, for wellnigh half a year, because he had uttered certain gross and harsh words to a certain minister of his. He would not allow his son to enter his sight until he had made satisfaction to the said minister.' The King refused to see Edward and forbade the officials of his household or the Exchequer to advance his son any money for the upkeep of his Court. Poor Edward for at least a month, in an attempt to regain the King's favour, followed him wherever he went 'at a distance of ten or twelve leagues', from Midhurst to Chichester, through Surrey and Kent to Canterbury. Edward spoke of 'the anguish which we have endured, and still suffer daily, through the ordinance and pleasure of our Lord the King'. Finally, a reconciliation took place at Westminster on the vigil of the Feast of the Translation of Edward the Confessor. One of the first things Edward II did after becoming King was to have the 'said minister' arrested and thrown into prison.

'He would not allow his son to enter his sight'

Edward I did not mellow with age, but he deteriorated. His second wife Margaret, sister of Philip the Fair, tried to protect his children, especially Edward, from their father's severity. The sisters were seldom there to give the young Prince help or advice, although he came to see more of Elizabeth and Joan who had both recently remarried, the former to Humphrey de Bohun, Earl of Hereford, and the latter to Ralph of Monthermer, a *mésalliance* which the King had reluctantly sanctioned. These two spirited daughters tended to get their own way with their father by using the often employed techniques of flirtatiousness and cajolery.

The next row between the King and his son was on the subject of Gavaston. The young Edward had gone to the limits of his own resources in enriching his friend and he needed his father's help to do more. He proposed that Gavaston be given the county of Ponthieu which he had inherited from his mother. This is how, in the words of the chronicler Hemingburgh, the King reacted to the suggestion. 'You baseborn whoreson, do you want to give away lands now, you who never gained any?' Seizing the Prince's hair in both hands, he tore out as much as he could until, exhausted, he drove him from his presence. After that he ordered Gavaston's expulsion from England.

The King did not live much longer after this scene with his son. The Scottish campaign started again, Edward I died attending to the business of the realm. Edward II, reacting against his father's highmindedness, lost no time in enjoying his liberty.

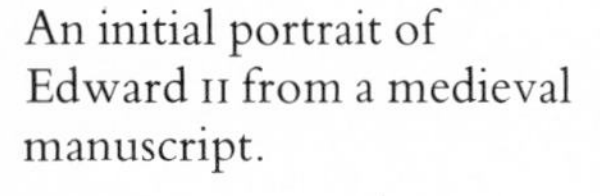

An initial portrait of Edward II from a medieval manuscript.

Within a few days of the King's death, his favourite was recalled from exile, and the Scottish campaign abandoned. Edward II reminds us of that other king, Edward VIII, who also refused to subordinate his 'pleasure' to his obligations. This has been their offence at the bar of history. The first Edward can be criticised for many things, but not for having failed to do his duty.

Historians used to delight in pointing out the contrasts between the character of the 'greatest of the Plantagenets' and his perverted, weakling son. We can now see that Edward II's inheritance was much less enviable than his father's had been. Edward's projects at the time of his death were so grandiose and expensive, that the most competent and dutiful son would have had difficulty in fulfilling them. 'Probably no medieval king left his finances in a more hopeless confusion than did the great Edward. Certainly none of them ever handed to his successor so heavy a task with such inadequate means to discharge it.'

Lanercost Priory, not far from Carlisle, where Edward I died on 7 July 1307.

Chronology

1215 Magna Carta
Fourth Lateran Council
1216 Henry III comes to the throne
1238 Simon de Montfort marries Eleanor, sister of Henry III
1239 Birth of Edward I
1240 Death of Llewelyn ap Iorwerth, the Great
1245 Henry III starts rebuilding Westminster Abbey
1247 Treaty of Woodstock between Henry III and Llewelyn ap Gruffydd
1249 St Louis' first Crusade begins
Alexander III becomes King of Scotland
1250 Death of the Emperor Frederick II
Henry III takes the Cross
St Louis captured in Egypt at Battle of Mansourah
1253 Henry III goes to Gascony
1254 Death of Emperor Conrad IV
Pope Innocent IV offers Crown of Sicily to Edmund of Lancaster
Edward given Wales, Chester, Gascony, etc. by his father Henry III
Edward marries Eleanor of Castile
Death of Innocent IV. Alexander IX becomes Pope
1257 Richard of Cornwall elected King of the Romans
1258 Conclusion of Sicilian Business
The Provisions of Oxford. Outbreak of baronial revolt
1259 Treaty of Paris
1260 Henry repudiates the Provisions of Oxford
1264 Mise or Award of Amiens. St Louis pronounces against the barons
Battle of Lewes. Edward becomes a hostage of the barons
1265 The Great Parliament
Edward escapes from the barons
Battle of Evesham. Simon de Montfort killed and the baronial revolt collapses
1267 Peace of Montgomery
1268 Edward takes the Cross
The fall of Antioch
1270 Edward goes on Crusade
Death of St Louis in Tunis. Philip III becomes King of France
Edward reaches crusaders' camp in Carthage
1271 Edward lands at Acre
1272 Death of Richard of Cornwall
Truce with Baibars, Sultan of Egypt
Edward sets sail from Acre for Sicily
Death of Henry III. Edward I proclaimed King
1273 The 'Little Battle of Châlons'
Edward does homage to Philip III for Gascony
Edward visits Gascony
1274 Edward returns to England
Edward and Eleanor crowned in Westminster Abbey
Robert Burnell becomes Chancellor
1275 Edward's first Parliament. First Statute of Westminster
1276 First Welsh war breaks out
1278 Statute of Gloucester
1279 Statute of Mortmain
1279 John Peckham becomes Archbishop of Canterbury
1282 Uprising in Wales led by David, Llewelyn ap Gruffydd's brother. Llewelyn killed
1284 Statute of Wales
Birth of Edward of Caernarvon
1285 Statute of Winchester
Second Statute of Westminster, *De Donis Conditionalibus*
Death of Philip III. Philip IV, the Fair, becomes King of France
1286 Edward goes to Gascony
1289 Edward returns from Gascony
1290 Edward expels all Jews from England
Third Statute of Westminster, *Quia Emptores* and *Quo Warranto*
Death at sea of Maid of Norway
Death of Eleanor of Castile
Treaty with Scotland

1291 Debate on the Great Cause opens at Norham
Death of Eleanor of Provence

1292 Death of John Peckham. Robert Winchelsey becomes Archbishop of Canterbury
Edward awards Scottish Crown to John Balliol

1293 British ships destroy Norman fleet off Brittany

1294 Boniface VIII becomes Pope
Philip IV attacks Gascony
Revolt breaks out in Wales
English expedition sent to Gascony
Alliance between Edward and Rhineland princes

1295 Balliol summoned to Westminster
'Auld Alliance' between France and Scotland
The 'Model' Parliament

1296 Abdication of John Balliol
Pope Boniface VIII issues bull, *Clericis Laicos*, forbiding taxation of the clergy

1297 William Wallace leads rebellion in Scotland in the name of Balliol and recovers most of the country
Edward makes alliance with Count of Flanders
Edward surrenders to baronial demands at Ghent

1298 Edward defeats the Scots at the Battle of Falkirk

1299 Edward marries Margaret, sister of Philip IV of France

1301 The young Edward given Wales and Chester

1302 Boniface VIII issues bull, *Unam Sanctam*

1303 Peace treaty between England and France. Philip withdraws from Gascony to England

1305 Clement V becomes Pope
Wallace captured and executed

1306 All Jews expelled from France
Rebellion in Scotland led by Robert Bruce

1307 Philip IV suppresses the Order of the Knights Templar
Edward dies at Burgh-upon-Sands on his way to Scotland

Select Bibliography

F. Barlow, *Edward the Confessor* (1970)
C. Bemont, *Simon de Montfort* (1930)
M. Beresford, *New Towns of the Middle Ages* (1967)
C. N. L. Brooke, *From Alfred to Henry III* (1960)
H. M. Colvin (ed.), *The History of the King's Works* (1964)
J. G. Edwards, *Edward I's Castle-Building in Wales* (1946)
H. Johnstone, *Edward of Caernarvon, 1284–1307* (1946)
M. Labarge, *Gascony, England's First Colony* (1980)
Simon de Montfort (1962)
W. R. Lethaby, *Westminster Abbey and the Kings' Craftsmen* (1906)
E. C. Lodge, *Gascony under English Rule* (1926)
Sir H. Maxwell (ed.), *The Chronicle of Lanercost, 1272–1346* (1913)
J. E. Morris, *The Welsh Wars of Edward I* (1901)
F. T. Plucknett, *Legislation of Edward I* (1949)
Sir M. Powicke, *Henry III and the Lord Edward*, 2 vols (1947)
The Thirteenth Century (1953)
M. Prestwich, *The Three Edwards* (1980)
C. W. Previte-Orton, *A History of Europe, 1198–1378* (1937)
H. Rothwell (ed.), *English Historical Documents 1189–1327*
Sir S. Runciman, *A History of the Crusades*, Vol. 3 (1954)
L. F. Salzman, *Edward I* (1968)
E. L. G. Stones and G. G. Simpson, *Edward I and the Throne of Scotland, 1290–6*, 2 vols. (1978)
W. Stubbs, *Historical Introductions to the Rolls Series* (1902)
Select Charters of English Constitutional History (1870)
A. J. Taylor, 'Edwardian Castles in Wales', *Proceedings of the British Academy* (1963)
F. Trautz, *Die Könige von England und das Reich, 1272–1377* (1961)
R. F. Treharne, *The Baronial Plan of Reform, 1258–63* (1932)
T. F. Tout, *The Place of the Reign of Edward II in English History* (1914)

Index